Servers of the Divine Plan

Servers of the Divine Plan

The Destiny of Ages is Nigh

Third Edition

RMB 817
Nannup, WA 6275
AUSTRALIA

E-mail: thenewcall@thenewcall.org
www.thenewcall.org

First published in 1999.

First Esoteric Publishing edition—2004

Published by Esoteric Publishing
PO Box 300249
Escondido CA 92030-0249

www.esotericpublishing.com

Printed in Canada

ISBN 1-889280-30-5

This book is dedicated to all those intrepid souls who have sacrificed their exulted spiritual freedom in voluntary service to humanity and planet Earth at this time of great need.

Contents

Foreword

THIS WORK IS NOT THE RESULT OF CHANNELLING (medium-ship), but is the product of a continuing and natural process of *remembrance* which has been expedited by our own uncompromising and full-time search across four continents from 1990 to 1999. During that period we left not one stone unturned in our ardent quest to uncover the genuine truth of the times and to solve the enigma of our growing and peculiar inner senses and spiritual experiences.

The information revealed in this book will be of interest and especial benefit to certain individuals who are beginning to penetrate the *veil of forgetfulness*, which has been necessarily imposed upon them by their own divine intelligence and by the laws pertaining to incarnation on Earth. Specifically addressed are those individuals who are presently undergoing the foreordained process of remembrance themselves, and who, in being stimulated by the rising frequencies of Aquarian energy, are becoming aware of the duty and service that they came to render at this time upon Earth and which, in turn, is the purpose of their incarnation.

However, the message contained within these pages is not exclusive. This book may benefit everyone alike because the process of transformation and awakening that is being exemplified by certain unique groups of souls in physical embodiment today parallels that which all humanity must undergo in order to be eligible to enter the New World, the birth of which is now very close.

The truth revealed herein contains catalytic seeds which, when recognized by those who are able, may serve to rekindle vague soul-memories and so contribute toward spiritual reorientation and awakening. Such awakening is both timely and necessary today, for we have arrived at a most critical juncture in the onward journey of both our planet and mankind. The planetary deadline for the advent of an unprecedented spiritual consciousness on Earth is imminent, and all who would gain access to the Portal leading into the New World are now being called to awaken and to arise in readiness to assist those amongst humanity who will accompany them.

A growing percentage of the human population are today remembering something of the intelligent design and infallibility of the Divine Plan for Earth at this time and their role to play in it. It is in such remembrance that we wish to fulfil our duty to all people in every part of the world, and we are especially devoted to helping in the recalling process for those who came specifically to aid humanity and the planet through the impending Great Transition.

Our long, dark night is almost over. Very soon, all awakened souls will unite again as one to greet the New Dawn, and to finally release that Grand Song which has been composed within their hearts during the course of many incarnations of personal sacrifice. It is our prayer that all servants of the race may now step forward to faithfully and confidently pool energies and resources so that together we may make haste toward the fulfilment of prophecy by consciously assisting in the predestined emergence of the New World Consciousness upon Earth.

* * *

When preparing a volume of this nature there are more unusual and unpredictable influences to contend with than is normally so. Similarly, the reader may experience certain difficulties in clearly grasping some of the fundamental verities revealed within this text. For example, drowsiness may be experienced by some, an inexplicable aversion to certain ideas may be observed by others, or perhaps a curious inability to assimilate new yet simple concepts. There may be three distinct reasons for this.

Firstly, certain truths conveyed in this book will present a significant moral challenge to some people, and so may evoke strong psycho-emotional reactions. Upon the spiritual path, old habit patterns, redundant belief systems and erroneous ideas that no longer serve the aspirant must first rise to the surface and present themselves to the conscious mind in order to be acknowledged, processed, resolved and upgraded so that a new and brighter life-perspective may be adopted. For the average person this necessary process of spiritual growth may trigger a degree of perplexity on various levels, and the reader may wish to bear in mind that bewilderment is often a natural symptom of inner purification. A very wise man once averred that: *"... the truth shall set you free."* However, challenge and struggle will always arise preceding greater spiritual freedom; such is a basic fact of life.

Secondly, certain concepts herein will undoubtedly compel some readers to think in a very different way to which they may be accustomed. This will have a similar effect upon one's mental faculty as that of exerting the physical body when it is not used to rigorous exercise: the muscles will easily tire. As is the case with physical training, perseverance is required if progress is to be made, and the dedicated student will find that his efforts pay commensurate dividends.

Thirdly, there exist antagonistic minds in the unseen worlds who definitely do not wish the contents of this volume to be revealed to anyone, anywhere, under any circumstances, at any time. Such intelligences work surreptitiously and, from hidden quarters, they may easily interfere with a person's perception and ability to comprehend. To the intelligent and tenacious, these discarnate souls can be at worst a trifle irksome, and the undesirable effects of all efforts made by such uninvited guests may be minimized and even nullified altogether by the steadfast application of one's will, against which they are impotent.

It is not uncommon for all three of the above complications to affect the reader to some degree and simultaneously, thereby inhibiting the light of new understanding. Nevertheless, should persistence be applied upon this important voyage of discovery, the rewards will far outweigh any difficulties that may be experienced throughout the venture. It is our earnest wish that all humanity may discover the whole truth with regard to the very unique spiritual opportunity that is available today to every sane and thinking person in the world, and may that truth liberate mankind once and for all from the illusion of separation and from suffering.

Who are the Servers?

IT IS NO SECRET TODAY to the enquiring or observant mind that momentous and unprecedented changes are transpiring within the solar system and upon Earth as the old Piscean era yields to the new Aquarian age. We are living in a period of radical purification and transformation in which everything is moving, changing, becoming. All peoples in every country of the world are presently experiencing the leading waves of a tremendous release of divine force upon Earth. An unparalleled global metamorphosis is now underway which is accelerating all-round human development, bringing major changes to Earthly life, and will presently lift humanity into a new era of advanced experience and expression as a New World is born.

Such a unique occasion is attracting the interest and attention of many other beings within the vast universe, and since planet Earth holds a key position in the local solar system and the galaxy as a whole, our globe has become a busy nucleus or intersection for much *traffic* from other planets, worlds and densities.* Members of various interstellar confederations—many of whom have their corresponding representatives in physical incarnation upon Earth at this time—have moved closer to our planet in order to assist with the now imminent Great Transition which shall positively affect all life on our world. The cry of humanity has been received, and loving support goes where it is required or earnestly requested.

Those whom we have called *Servers* emanate from other more highly evolved world systems where the general spiritual development has reached such a level that unconditional love and fellow-

---

* The term 'density' denotes a vibrational frequency of consciousness or plane of existence. The occult structure of the lower part of the universe in which we reside—the *Cosmic Physical Plane*—is most often described using a septenary model, i.e., seven ascending levels from the most dense or most material at the bottom level to the least dense or quickest vibration at the top. Each major level, or plane, can then be divided again into seven sub-levels. However, such clear-cut divisions are for conceptual convenience only, for, in truth, one level cannot really be distinguished from the next since the whole spectrum of vibratory frequencies changes by extremely subtle gradations. The most prevalent level of consciousness amongst the mass of human beings on.

ship are spontaneously known and expressed. Many of these Servers are members of advanced civilizations that have achieved and maintained a far greater alignment with the divine Will than humanity and so have realized a much higher degree of rapport with the Universal Purpose, as well as unity of thought and activity with one another. In order to honour their voluntary commitment which was made to humanity long ago, some of these advanced beings have been taking human embodiments upon Earth for millions of years; others have presently offered their service to mankind in incarnation for the very first time; still others have opted not to utilize physical bodies at all and remain resident within the hidden worlds, yet in close attendance to our planet, working, watching, waiting and answering calls for assistance sounded by those in incarnation upon Earth who invoke their aid with unselfish motives and intelligent intent.

There are many and diverse classes of Servers who have taken human incarnation upon Earth today and who derive from the inner or higher planes of various star systems. These dedicated and dutiful agents of goodwill have volunteered to descend into the more dense spheres of our planetary body in order to lead humanity in a very important task. Not all of these emissaries are ordinary individual souls. In addition to a large number of *group-souls* and hierarchies of divine envoys who have necessarily divided their ranks in order to serve in individualized incarnation, there exist also upon Earth carefully selected elements of great multidimensional beings, or *ultraterrestrials*, who principally and customarily function as one cosmic mind amongst a vast multitude of similar collective entities that operate throughout various worlds and densities spanning the universe. Like many tiny sparks sent forth from a great ethereal blaze, such exalted lives have chosen to temporarily fragment their unity in order to diffuse their service throughout certain lower-vibratory frequencies of the Cosmos, and to ultimately take physical embodiment upon our planet. This is a great act of compassion indeed, yet one which is deemed by these sublime intelligences to be most necessary at this important stage of Earth's spiritual development, and one which shall yield very positive consequences, the like of which humanity has never before witnessed throughout its entire history.

Those Servers who have taken numerous previous incarnations upon Earth have, in past, repeatedly struggled with the burdens, the dangers, the sorrows and the pain of everyday terrestrial living; in being confronted by all its peculiar trials and challenges, they have wrestled and fought for justice upon our planet. Collectively, they have trodden every step of the way of suffering, have undergone every mundane and psychical experience, have surmounted every difficulty, and have endured. These servants of the race have, many times, known the immolation of the personal or lower self; they are the martyrs and saints of yesteryear, and know well, therefore, that complete renouncement of every worldly value, an unconditional repudiation of all non-essentials, which is also the prescription for all truly spiritually-aspiring souls on Earth at this time. There is no adversity, no sacrifice, no bitter personal loss which they have not, in their time, experienced. They have explored all the avenues of knowledge available on Earth, descended into the deepest valleys of life and into the darkest depths of hell. From there they have climbed to the mountain top of spiritual accomplishment and have then proceeded to transcend both space and time, losing all identification with the individual self to become but focussed points of light in the Universal Mind; and herein lies their qualification to serve mankind, for today they are back among us, to help.

Knowing, therefore, the quintessence of pain, and comprehending thoroughly the possible depths of sin and suffering attainable by humanity, the Servers' methods can be perfectly gauged to individual needs. Yet at the same time their realization of the liberation to be achieved during this critical period—the end of a major world cycle—and their apprehension of the greater freedom that is assured through the rejection of the old and outmoded ways of life in exchange for the emerging new world paradigm, suffices to give them a complete understanding of the present needs of the human race.

Awakening Servers upon the planet today are generally characterized by an ardent and purposeful love which, in regard to the good of the whole, is uncompromising. They may be identified by a spiritual intelligence that has been gained through countless Earthly and extraterrestrial lives in which they have worked their way from the bottom of life and of evolution well nigh to their final emancipation from matter, soon to be realized by some of them. They are to be recognized by their depth of experience which has been forged by time itself together with a multiplicity of interactions with numerous and diverse life-forms, and by a courage and commitment that is the result of that experience, and which, having been produced by ages of endeavour, failure, and renewed endeavour, and having in the long run led to victory, can again today be placed at the feet of humanity in world service.

Those particular Servers who have become well-acquainted with life on Earth have cultivated an ability to persist even when they may seem to have undergone more than sufficient suffering, and they know a determination that triumphs over all setbacks, for it is founded upon a long-cultivated patience, extensive experience and divine Purpose. They may, therefore, also be recognized by their one-pointed dedication, which is both enlightened and intelligent and which is cooperative, adjusting itself to the immediate requirements of the human race, and thus fitting in with the current designs of the Divine Plan for Earth.

One might understandably ask the question: if there is indeed so much struggle, hardship and suffering involved in the Servers' physical-plane activity, why then do they not refrain from incarnating upon Earth at all, and simply help the world from the subtle planes by 'working from home,' as it were? There are two main reasons for the Servers' physical presence upon the planet. Firstly, and most importantly, they incarnate in the physical world in order that archetypal ideas—carefully formulated within the Divine Mind— may be lived out by them on the plane of matter, and so be brought into manifestation in human consciousness. Once these archetypal ideas have been introduced to the consciousness of the race by being realized and lived by persons who form a part of that consciousness, they are caught up by humanity and become an integral part of its collective awareness and life-paradigm.

Secondly, Servers in physical incarnation are able to offer certain forms of assistance that incorporeal spiritual guides upon the inner planes cannot. For example, and due to their physical existence, Servers in Earthly embodiment possess the ability to contact humanity externally. Consequently, they are much more likely to find that their aid is received by those who are unable to be contacted by the invisible helpers of the race upon the inner or hidden side of life; their love may be welcomed by those who remain sceptical about the subtle worlds. It should be understood, however, that such succor given individually is but a tiny part of the overall duty of Servers, and presently the greater collective mission will unfold itself, as results derived from the Great Work of Ages begin to manifest upon Earth.

Many Servers who have incarnated primarily to aid in humanity's transition at this time are just now, today, becoming aware of the close attendance of a vast array of Cosmic Intelligences who are hidden to most, the exalted ranks to which they inherently belong.

As vague yet familiar senses begin to form within their minds in accord with a predetermined and revolutionary process of remembrance that is presently being accelerated throughout the world, these Servers are beginning to consciously feel a sense of enormous purpose and urgency in their lives. Their necessarily imposed veil of forgetfulness is being lifted today by unseen hands, and their memories and higher spiritual faculties are returning to them.

The Servers are reawakening in preparation for the execution of a grand and noble work, the ramifications of which bear universal significance. They are beginning to recall the purpose of their duty to humanity and to planet Earth, and are remembering that they are an essential part of a vast, collective effort and a tremendously important task, the scope of which stretches back across millions of years and a myriad of past incarnations upon Earth and elsewhere, all geared toward the now imminent and conclusive glory. In their partial remembrance thus far, the Servers are perceiving with great felicity that they are about to realize the grand consummation of a vital phase of the Divine Plan for Earth, the solar system and beyond, the result of which shall cast life-enhancing reverberations throughout the universe.

Past and Future

I tell you that the children of yesteryear are walking in the funeral of the era which they created for themselves. They are pulling a rotting rope that may break soon and cause them to drop into a forgotten abyss. I say that they are living in homes with weak foundations. As the storm blows — and it is about to blow — their homes will fall upon their heads and thus become their tombs. I say that all their thoughts, their sayings, their quarrels, their compositions, their books and all their works are nothing but chains dragging them because they are too weak to pull the load.

But the children of tomorrow are the ones called by life, and they follow it with steady steps and heads high. They are the dawn of the new frontiers; no smoke will veil their eyes and no jingle of chains will drown out their voices. They are few in number but the difference is as between a grain of wheat and a stack of hay. No one knows them but they know each other. They are like the summits, which can see and hear each other — not like caves, which cannot hear or see. They are the seed dropped by the hand of God in the field, breaking through its pod and waving its sapling leaves before the face of the sun. It shall grow into a mighty tree; its roots in the heart of the Earth and its branches high in the sky.

Kahlil Gibran

The Purpose of Incarnating Servers

IN ORDER TO GAIN A BASIC OVERVIEW of the origins of the pattern of migrating helpers of the race, something of the genesis and development of modern man needs to be understood.

Ages ago, when Earth's primates had not yet evolved into bipedal self-conscious creatures, celestial co-creators came to this planet and seeded a variety of new humanoid races (as well as a miscellany of vegetable and animal life) as part of a great experiment. This well-intentioned intervention from the stars unfolded over an extended period of time and at different points all around the planet under the direction of technologically and spiritually advanced representatives of diverse worlds situated at various locations in the universe. Thus the process of genetic co-creation was of considerable complexity in which many civilizations were involved and who still today maintain an active interest and karmic investment in a multitude of life-forms upon Earth, including mankind. The principal idea of the planetary experiment with regard to humanity was to create a race of great diversity that would so develop as to eventually express a truly divine consciousness upon the physical plane, and so demonstrate love, wisdom and spiritual intelligence upon what was then known as the 'Jewel of the Solar System': *Terran* or planet Earth.

It was thus, far back in time, that a karmic link was established between these interstellar progenitors and humanity, a relationship not unlike that between parents and their children, and consequently those who were responsible for the creation of modern humankind have since been actively and lovingly protecting and serving their 'offspring,' sometimes even incarnating into human bodies themselves in order to further the planetary experiment and to aid in the upliftment of consciousness upon Earth. Since its emergence from out of primeval antiquity, however, humanity has succeeded in attracting to itself various other Guardians and Benefactors in addition to its original parents,[*] and it will be presently seen that mankind has never really been alone upon this tiny planet floating on the edge of the Milky Way.

Approximately 18 million years ago, in the middle of the Lemurian

---

[*] It should be mentioned that the ignorance and selfishness demonstrated by mankind over the ages has also invited to Earth numerous alien groups of a decidedly belligerent and tyrannical nature. These warlords also created certain races of human beings. As fascinating as this particular subject is, however, it is beyond the scope of the present volume.

epoch, the general Plan for the unfoldment of consciousness of all life on Earth, including humanity, was entrusted to a group of spiritual luminaries emanating chiefly from the advanced civilization of Venus who accepted the duties and responsibilities of Earth's new inner planetary government, and who have been directing and aiding our world ever since. This great body of Lords, Masters and Initiates is frequently and reverently referred to as *The Great White Brotherhood,*[*] *The Christ-Hierarchy* or simply *The Planetary or Spiritual Hierarchy,* and some among them have also repeatedly incarnated upon the physical planet in the past in order to effect certain vital functions. Today, in line with the present occasion and need, certain members of the Earth's Hierarchy of Great Souls are again taking physical incarnation, and in unprecedented numbers.

Furthermore, during the long history of the human race on Earth, in addition to the loving guidance of the planetary Hierarchy and in response to invocations from various practising occult bodies upon the planet, other very advanced entities from multifarious origins throughout the Cosmos have also attempted to give spiritual assistance to humanity at different times. Such counsel in the past, however, nearly always became distorted by the grasping and misconceiving minds of mankind, which proceeded to exploit higher truths and mystical secrets for selfish purposes. The eventual fall of Atlantis and ancient Egypt are typical results of this repetitive pattern. In fact, the repeated misuse of human free will has so distorted and corrupted the intended design for mankind's harmonious spiritual development that our globe has today come to be known as 'the dark planet' by various sentient lives with whom we share our universe, for the original Divine Plan for Earth has gone awry. Consequently, our cosmic ancestors as well as the aforementioned auxiliary Servers have moved closer to the planet at this time and are today attempting to help humanity back onto its destined path, while restoring the integrity of their past teachings (as well as updating them), and simultaneously offering further assistance wherever it is earnestly sought.

The majority of records describing visitations from and communications with such 'god-like' beings have been destroyed in the past by natural disasters and by evil forces working through the reckless egotism of

---

[*]   Numerous volumes have been written about the Great White Brotherhood and the level of spiritual attainment, duties, activities, etc. of its members. Much of this material may be obtained from the *Theosophical Society.* It is recommended that serious students avail themselves of a basic understanding of the structure and general function of the planetary Hierarchy, which is too large a subject to be dealt with here.

misguided and fanatical religious missionaries, conquerors and pious tyrants. Yet clues still remain to be seen, for example in Mexico, South America and Australia; meanwhile intriguing but previously lost or hidden historical information is resurfacing in the world today, and for very good reasons, for humanity is at last being primed to receive and understand the whole truth!

A relatively small number amongst the ranks of Servers who have incarnated upon Earth during the past have done so in order to anchor certain energies into the planetary consciousness, and to thereby maintain some awareness upon the planet regarding the destiny of humanity, a very important and intermediate phase of which shall be known at the completion of the present world sub-cycle: the Piscean age. Theirs has been a strictly holy work, while a far greater number of 'lesser' *servants of God* have become prominently successful as innovators, reformers and leaders, conscientiously inspiring mankind and generally contributing toward the expansion and progress of human consciousness. Some have named these Servers 'The Starseed,' denoting that their origins are other than Earthly,[*]

---

[*]   In truth, the vast majority of souls presently in human incarnation upon Earth have not originated or evolved from the lower kingdoms of this planet (i.e., from its mineral, vegetable and animal evolutions) as may be the case for the native 'animal-man' who is still to be found today constituting certain primitive tribes in Africa, South America, etc. Therefore, the soul who is a member of modern humanity might also be regarded as a 'visitor' to Earth. However, the term 'starseed' includes certain classes of migrating souls who are *not* here today on Earth primarily to serve. A far greater proportion of starseeds have been and continue to be attracted to this planet in order to *learn* from the Earth experiment, to balance their own karma, and some arrive here for far more sinister purposes! Therefore, many starseeds actually contribute towards the problems on Earth due to their own ignorance, even though that ignorance may be of a uniquely extraterrestrial or starry nature! Our term, 'Server,' refers to a soul who has been charged with a specifically beneficent assignment upon the planet that is in alignment with the Divine Plan, and who has also successfully managed—perhaps during numerous Earthly lifetimes of serviceful activity—to remain free of becoming 'Earth-bound,' i.e., karmically tied to the ordinary rounds of human incarnation. A starseed, therefore, is not necessarily a Server. A greater appreciation of these esoteric concepts, together with their various implications, may be gained by reading further.

and many incarnating *seeds* throughout Earth's history have helped to secure the now imminent successful germination of an unparalleled spiritual epoch for humanity: the birth of a New World Consciousness.

However, as previously stated, and due to various negative influences such as frequent interference by *cosmic evil*, the original Plan has not unfolded in the way that was anticipated, either by the early co-creators or by humanity's more recently appointed Guardians: the Spiritual Hierarchy. Since our planet is vitally connected to and therefore affects the progress of many other world systems in the galaxy, this situation has created a much greater requirement for additional divine assistance, and the numbers of Servers who are in attendance on Earth today, both embodied and incorporeal, has increased substantially in order to meet this important need and to restore balance upon an imprisoned planet that has strayed so far from universal law and which has consequently become near-saturated with ignorance, karma and the tyranny of evil intent.

In order to grasp an even deeper understanding of the purposes of and requirements for the greater influx of incarnating Servers at this time, it will be helpful to consider something of the present status, intent and mode of operation of the Earth's own planetary Hierarchy, the functions and purposes of which are reflected both upwards and down throughout many different spheres of universal life: *"As above, so below."* Like mankind, the planetary Hierarchy is itself presently at a point of spiritual crisis. Many of its members now stand before the Portal that leads to the Way of the Higher Evolution, and the entire personnel of the Earth-Hierarchy is patiently waiting to make a united move forward, paralleling—on its own level—the move forward that humanity is about to take.

Now, under the Law of Synthesis, mankind's spiritual Elders are able to move forward and upward only in so far as their efforts encompass all densities down to and including the physical plane. Humanity and its Hierarchy of Great Souls are essentially inseparable; the efforts, successes or failures of one inevitably affect the other. Hence the necessity for the incarnation upon Earth of members of the Guardians of the race, and the demonstration of their united ability to work from the physical plane all the way up to the highest in order to move collectively through the succeeding portal and further along the Way.

Much earlier this century, having surveyed the maturity of consciousness and, therefore, the spiritual potential of humanity, some members of the spiritual Hierarchy instigated an innovative and enthusiastic proposal to incarnate upon the physical plane in order to expedite the inevitable process of world initiation, and for the first time in such numbers since their last major incarnation during Atlantean days. However, their hopes did not go according to plan, principally due to the lack of cooperation by humanity itself, the heart and minds of which have been kept under the sway of materialism, selfishness, separation and fear. Secularism and self-seeking still predominate upon Earth today, and so the required and favorable conditions that the planetary Hierarchy had wished to instigate in order that certain members could externalize themselves in the physical world, have not been brought about. It was consequently decided by humanity's Elders that further help was required, and this is another reason for the great increase of interstellar Servers at this important juncture of Earth's onward journey.

The Call was sounded, and today the positive response is being felt. Approaching the Earth from a multitude of regions throughout numerous worlds and dimensions, Servers incarnate voluntarily bearing a complete propensity toward helpfulness, the most vital aspects of which are intended to be rendered at the appropriate time and in certain ways unique to each Server or group of Servers, but always in compliance with the Divine Plan for mankind and the planet. From one perspective, such a departure from their celestial home and projection outward into the far grosser densities of Earth might be regarded as a tremendous act of sacrifice, yet it would be more spiritually correct to say that such a going forth is a profound gesture of love for humanity and its planet.

The following poem by Paramahansa Yogananda—who was himself a devoted servant of the race—expresses succinctly the love and attitudes of all awakened Servers of the Divine Plan:

God's Boatman

I want to ply my boat, many times,
Across the gulf after death,
And return to Earth's shores,
From my home in Heaven.
I want to load my boat,
With those waiting, thirsty ones,
Who are left behind,
And carry them by the opal pool,
Of iridescent joy,
Where my Father distributes,

His all-desire-quenching liquid peace.
Oh, I will come again and again!
Crossing a million crags of suffering;
With bleeding feet I will come,
If need be, a trillion times,
So long as I know,
One stray brother is left behind.
I want Thee, Oh Lord,
That I may give Thee to all.
Free me, then, Oh God,
From the bondage of the body,
That I may show others,
How they can free themselves.
I want Thine everlasting bliss,
Only that I may share it with others;
That I may show all my brothers,
The way to happiness,
Forever and forever, in Thee.

✳ ✳ ✳

The spiritual level attained by the various types of Servers, their unique origins, and their particular, individual purposes and expressions upon Earth range within a very broad spectrum, and the specific classification of even a fraction of these details presents a most daunting if not impossible task. However, it may be generally stated that the (re-)incarnation of the more accomplished Servers today is not necessitated due to personal karma, nor is it inspired solely by their desire for experience, as is usual for most Earth-bound souls as they proceed upon the regular cycles of karmic learning and reconciliation.

In addition to those Servers who have in past been summoned to Earth and who have responded positively by visiting this planet before, what might be termed 'emergency recruits' have only recently been entreated by a call for further assistance sounded by active Servers themselves who have recognized that many members among their own ranks upon Earth have been unable to rise above the planet's negative influences and have consequently lost sight of their purpose in incarnation. Due to the fact that so many needed Servers have, during the last few decades, been distracted from their mission, delay in the manifestation of the Divine Plan for Earth has resulted, causing much dire inconvenience to certain aspects of its schedule. The world-ego is well-practised in its designs, and today continues to work insidiously toward hindering and subduing potential instruments of divine service in the world.

All Servers have been called to assist in the urgent process of global cleansing by elevating the planetary consciousness in preparation for humanity's emergence into the Aquarian age. Therefore, it can be seen that the overall objective of Servers at this critical time is to raise the planetary vibration and thus to stimulate human consciousness so that mankind may more readily make contact with the world of spiritual ideas and henceforth cooperate with the Divine Plan. Success in such an effort will result in humanity's positive orientation toward that which is currently of moment in the world, the intelligent acceptance of today's great challenges and opportunities, and the consequent transformation of global awareness in preparation for the birth of the New World.

It is the duty of Servers to highlight the immediate circumstances with which humanity is confronted, and therefore to indicate the needed changes. In their task of catalyzing, stimulating and reorienting mankind back toward a realization of its innate divine nature (and consequently the very meaning of life), Servers strive to evoke higher aspiring attitudes and deeper spiritual understanding in a race that has long forgotten both its origins and purpose. By revealing the glories of the true vision of the Aquarian age and the imminent destiny for mankind, they seek to enkindle the smouldering embers of the world-soul which has become lost amidst nearly six billion bewildered personalities (not to mention the innumerable other incorporeal beings who reside within the subtle spheres of the planet). By offering contemporary truth, Servers attempt to fan the flame of the human spirit back to life, so that as many men and women as possible may be prepared to joyfully welcome to Earth the majesty of that which now lies just a little way ahead for the whole planet.

The zodiacal sign of Aquarius is the water carrier: a man who has on his shoulder a pitcher of water so full that it spills over, and yet the flow never diminishes. Awakened Servers—symbolically the water carriers of the Aquarian age—are able to tap the limitless source of divine Love, and, through their efforts to create a better world, allow this 'water of life' to flow to all who thirst.

The present-day duties of Servers may be concisely enumerated as follows:

1. To hold before the eyes of humanity the vision of the current phase of the Divine Plan for Earth.
2. To educate mankind regarding the most pertinent and urgent issues of the day.
3. To guide others toward a realization of their own innate divinity.
4. To inspire mankind to enter upon its destined work of planetary service.
5. To restore balance and, therefore, to help heal planet Earth.
6. To receive illumination from the higher worlds and to share this wherever appropriate for the furtherance of mankind's spiritual interests.
7. To act as a bridge between the old and the New—the lower and the Higher—by receiving light and power from above, and, using both of these under the inspiration of loving purpose, to eradicate evil, reinstate virtue, anchor the new Aquarian frequencies into the physical plane, and so help build the New World of tomorrow.

Presently, it is still the case that very few amongst humanity fully realize what is occurring in our solar system and upon the planet. They fail to really grasp the one true vision of the immediate future and do not truly see the beauty and magnitude of the emerging Plan. However, it is with that small percentage who are humbly aware of the import of the times and who will constitute the *critical mass* required to birth the New World Consciousness, that the Servers can work, because these individuals, even when lacking a thorough understanding, are able to recognize truth and purity of motive; they share the same sense of responsibility, appreciation of the impending, unprecedented spiritual opportunity and need for cooperation that is similarly felt by all awakening Servers today. It is intelligent altruism, selflessness and love that will be the calling cards of those members of humanity who shall arise with the Servers together as a group to greet the imminent New Dawn.

Judgement Day (the Harvest Time)

INSUPERABLE COSMIC FORCES began the prophesied acceleration and advancement of the Divine Plan for Earth much earlier
this century, but only relatively recently has this necessary process
been substantially hastened. By way of its more tangible effects,
therefore, it has attracted the attention of a larger percentage of the
world's population, and it is these more aware persons who are
responsible for introducing today's novel thought-trends, elaborate
cosmologies, expanded spiritual philosophies and new healing
modalities, which collectively have come to be regarded as the *New
Age movement*. The ongoing changes that are currently being so
avidly discussed and researched by those who belong to this movement represent a very important preliminary phase of the Divine
Plan for mankind at the end of this Piscean cycle, yet they constitute only an integral part of a much larger process, the concluding
stage of which, as far as humanity is presently concerned, has generally and metaphorically come to be known as 'Judgement Day.'
The destiny of every single soul upon Earth is inseparably linked
with this momentous and now impending time of critical human
choice and planetary transformation.

These culminating world events within the vast cycles and sub-
cycles of cosmic unfoldment have occurred many times during the
past and they will continue to take place whenever the dawn of a
major epoch is about to break. They present, therefore, in and of
themselves, nothing new, yet the great opportunity that is offered
to all life which they influence is unprecedented for that cycle.

Approximately every 25,000 years the hour of Judgement Day
strikes for planet Earth, and each 75,000-year period represents a
major cycle which yields its own major Judgement Day. These most
important occasions present great catalysts for the spiritual
advancement of accomplished souls, and some aware persons have
more aptly termed such a momentous period 'The Harvest Time,'
signifying that all those who have learned well the lessons of the
physical plane will be *harvested* into, or promoted to, a higher, more
expansive level of experience.

In the past, certain individuals have managed to harvest themselves early. These assiduous personalities have often been referred
to as 'enlightened,' and techniques of self-liberation, e.g., yoga,
meditation, etc. have addressed this possibility, although *sitting for
enlightenment* has ever been lengthy and difficult, and only those

15

persons possessing an indomitable will and unyielding diligence have succeeded. Today, however, at the end of this 75,000-year major cycle, and consequently due to the tremendous spiritual opportunity afforded each and every person on Earth, it is much easier for all humanity to ascend in consciousness, and groups of souls will be harvested during the birth of the New World in accordance with their ability to attune to the grace of the present period and to thereby succeed in raising the frequency of their consciousness, for the key to success at the Time of Harvest is *vibration*. Each individual's consciousness (which is an integral part of the planetary vibration) must be raised to a minimal level in order to qualify for graduation into the New World.

There are many legends of a 'Day of Judgement' at which time the future destiny of mankind is decided. Behind these legends there lies an important truth, although the fanciful imagination of certain religious adherents has, in the past, misinterpreted the perfectly simple and logical fact of necessary karmic reconciliation into a distorted and whimsical idea of 'everlasting damnation.' It is a perfect part of the Divine Plan that cosmic forces bring to an end cycles, ideologies, societies and civilizations when the due and right time comes. This is done in order to make place for that which is better and which will prove adequate, and not limiting, to the awakening consciousness and to the emerging life.

The Judgement Day as found in scriptural behests is a conveniently recallable simile for a necessary separation of souls, when human beings who are not sufficiently advanced to progress with the rest will be excluded from the ongoing stream of life. With regard to the imminent Judgement Day, divine ordinance will ensure that the development of such immature souls will continue upon another planet where conditions are better suited to their specific needs and more befitting to their level of evolvement.

Leading up to the 'Day of Reckoning' when the 'Book of Records' will be opened for everyone to see, all those who have failed to take full advantage of the spiritual opportunities afforded them during many lifetimes will depart from the rounds of Earthly incarnation where a more advanced life-expression is about to begin. However, this does not mean extinction or eternal damnation of the soul, even though it does impose a considerable though incalculable delay to its onward journey. While such delay is unquestionably serious, nevertheless the universal Law of Recompense knows no biased leniency and so can show no special sympathy for those who do not *make the grade*. Such underdeveloped souls are clearly in need of more experience upon the battlefield of physical-plane life, and that experience they will be given by law, even though it may mean innumerably additional lifetimes, many of which will include much suffering. Conversely, all those souls who successfully meet the greater requirements of the impending Harvest Time will be liberated from the *wheel of rebirth* and will be entirely free of the obligation to incarnate in any of the fallen worlds on any planet ever again.

So we may now recognize that, with regard to today's cyclic spiritual opportunity, there are three distinct groups:

i.   Those who, having failed to learn the lessons of the physical plane over many lifetimes, will be forced to leave the Earth in order to later incarnate on another physical world so that they may begin again to learn by way of the unique experiences and opportunities that are available only in the third density.

ii. Those who have learned sufficiently from and passed the tests of the physical-plane school and who will have therefore earned their promotion to the fourth- or fifth-density classroom of life where they shall proceed with their higher learning. However, it should be understood that such a graduation does not mean Liberation or Enlightenment, and the promoted soul will at some stage in the future be compelled by karmic law to return, via reincarnation, to the physical plane in order to once again attempt to achieve the one Goal of every unenlightened human being: *transfiguration,* or ultimate liberation from matter (including the more subtle matter of the 4th and 5th densities). Therefore, the graduation to the 4th or 5th densities is actually a temporary promotion into more rarefied spheres of existence and experience, and so may be termed 'the lesser harvest.'

iii. Those who have discovered and gone the Path of Return[*] and who are, therefore, able to be lifted up into the sixth cosmic sphere—the *Body of Christ*—and so who will attain the Final Liberation from all the lower worlds of fallen nature by being harvested back into the divine Kingdom. This is the true Harvest and has been the prime focus of all Avatars throughout human history.

---

[*]   The Path of Return and its requirements—scarcely known but vital esoteric information—is available to all earnest seekers. (See end of document)

Most Christians today do not fully realize that a vital part of the great mission of Jesus two thousand years ago was to attempt to prepare humanity for this present time of unprecedented planetary transformation and spiritual opportunity. It was with the objective of saving as many souls as possible from avoidable delay and suffering that the Piscean Christ said to his disciples: *"Go ye into all the world and preach the gospel to every creature; he that believeth and is baptized shall be saved, but he that believeth not shall be damned."* For baptism, and its corresponding rites in other religions, is a sign of the dedication of one's life in service to the Divine Plan and to humanity, and the one who grasps the truth of universal law, and so resolutely forgets the self in order to look forward and upward in the right direction, will certainly be amongst the *saved* who escape the *damnation* of the succeeding Judgement Day. The word 'damned' is indicative of the rejection from the present life-current which is about to be promoted, and a throwing back into the preceding of the successive life-streams; a veritable damnation indeed for all those who would prefer to move ahead spiritually and to behold the splendor of a new human consciousness and a new world.

After the Great Separation—the period of which Jesus referred to as *"The Sifting Time,"* what the Koran terms *"Qiyamat,"* and which immediately precedes the new era that the Mayan Prophecy calls *"The Golden Age"*—world conditions will be specially adapted for the rapid progress of the more advanced souls, and will therefore be wholly unsuitable for those who are at a much lower stage of development. The more intense frequencies of energy upon the planet in the future would not rouse the higher nature of the less-developed man, but would instead stimulate and amplify his lower passions, so that while he would not himself benefit by being on Earth at that time, he would also present difficulties for the progress of the more advanced souls. The New World stands ready and waiting today to admit humanity into its higher vibratory field of life, but those who have failed to learn the vital lessons which it has been their choice to learn or not to learn for many incarnations will be unable to venture forth due to incompatibility of vibration; such is a fundamental ruling decreed by the forthcoming Judgement Day.

* * *

Past examples of Harvest Times can be verified by referring to esoteric history. The great catastrophe that destroyed Atlantis many thousands of years ago was a veritable Judgement Day of a similar yet lesser order to that which is now impending, and which will, as it did in the end times of Atlantis, reject all those souls who are unqualified to proceed with the remainder of the race. It is probable that in Atlantean times, just as in our own, many or even most people failed to believe or heed the warning signs, their prophets or their predictions, yet today a little intelligent observation and research will highlight clearly to those who remain objective what shall be.

It is plainly evident to all of discerning awareness that, owing to their materialistic attitudes, those who cling to the old and outmoded ways of life will be unfit to continue side by side with the more spiritually-oriented population in the New World. Therefore, it may be seen just how critical it is in these times to subscribe sincerely and fully to all that is new, relevant and righteous, for the Harvest Time is at hand. A mere interest in the truth of the times is most definitely not sufficient. Cursory inquisitiveness never managed to raise anyone's vibration by very much and will certainly not, by itself, produce a positive result at the Time of Harvest. It is the *demonstration of love* alone that shall positively affect a person's consciousness. Therefore, active and altruistic response to the present need is demanded today in order for success to be known, not passive acquiescence.

Every candidate for graduation presently has both the marvellous opportunity and spiritual responsibility to his own soul for raising his consciousness as he may in these 'end times.' As new life-energies flood the planet, animating world awareness, every human being is faced with an important choice. Whether they wish to or not, whether they understand or not, each and every person will shortly be compelled to make a choice that will greatly affect both the present course of their spiritual development and their future, throughout incalculable incarnations. It must be emphasized that this choice will be determined by each man's *demonstration* of his decision. It will be his ability to express and, therefore, evidence his choice that will affect the vibratory rate of consciousness, and it is this which shall establish whether that person has opted to move forward with that which is new and vital, or whether he has chosen to remain a part of the old world consciousness which is today in a state of demise as preparations are made for its imminent and permanent elimination from planet Earth.

Opportunity to make a great leap in consciousness is presently being given, therefore, to those souls who possess reasonable potential for harvest. A system of 'privileged incarnation' for planet Earth was instigated several decades ago, and this has necessarily become more exacting recently as the Harvest Time draws nearer. Divine decree is today permitting a far greater incarnation than has been previously known of those souls whose chances of utilizing well contemporary life-experience upon the planet are most favorable, and this in order that they may become adequately prepared for success at the time of the Great Transition. This is one of the reasons that many children on Earth today are far more spiritually advanced than their parents and teachers. An overwhelming number of souls are eager for Earthly incarnation at this time due to the present unprecedented opportunity for rapid spiritual progress on the planet. At the time of writing (1997), there is a baby-boom occurring in various countries of the world. If human beings could but see and so fully appreciate the extremely good fortune in having a physical embodiment at this time upon Earth, then they might choose to appropriately adjust their attitudes to life, attune to the grace of the Aquarian energies, consequently guarantee their place amidst the successful entrants to the New World, and so abide in joyous anticipation of the forthcoming Final Liberation that has been promised to humanity since ancient times.

Servers, of course, qualify to be included within the privileged system of incarnation previously mentioned. In fact, most of them attained the minimum vibratory rate required for successful harvest from the third density into higher consciousness a long, long time ago, and they are here today solely to help others to do the same. Awakened Servers are, therefore, sometimes known as 'The Harvesters,' and this is because one of their principal duties is to reach out and help as many people as possible in order that a greater proportion of humanity may ready themselves for the approaching promotion into the New World. Therefore, it is not difficult to see how an individual's response to a Server's appeal today may determine that person's success at the forthcoming Harvest Time.

It has been estimated that the number of Servers present upon Earth today in physical incarnation exceeds one-hundred million, and this figure is ever increasing as more among their ranks are incarnating daily. Members of humanity who choose the path of conscious preparation will be automatically aided by the Servers, and together they will pass through the Portal of Initiation and into the New World. By offering a field of service, Servers provide the all-important opportunity for humanity to attain the preparatory requirements that will ensure their future success. They do this by offering contemporarily-relevant information, spiritual counsel and a worthy focus or life-aspiration, all of which are born from their own recognition of the truth of the times and, therefore, the need of the hour. Servers may thus be regarded as guides during the period leading up to the planetary deadline and the Harvest Time itself.

Servers, acting as custodians of the Divine Plan, give the final opportunity to humanity for redemption before the now impending Judgement Day; they are the 'messengers of God' spoken of in many different scriptural prophecies: *"Be not forgetful to entertain strangers, for thereby some have entertained angels unawares."*— Hebrews 13:2. The essential meaning of the word *'Angel'* is *divine messenger,* and all awakened Servers today are bearers of a most important message for humanity.

Looks can be deceiving, however, and some of the more highly evolved Servers upon Earth are extremely well camouflaged at this time in order that their advanced spiritual status remains undetected by the common man until the appropriate moment. Such latent instruments of grace presently express but a hint of the divine light that will shine forth when their true nature is revealed to the world. While awaiting the full arrival into the physical body of their divine soul, most often themselves as a personality unaware yet of exactly who they are, some Servers have even been diagnosed by an unsuspecting medical profession as retarded, autistic, etc., so thoroughly are they concealed. Yet when it is time for their full remembrance they will again resume their familiar task of working diligently with uncompromising dedication to the greatest good by offering perfectly appropriate spiritual guidance in the world. Such loving service will be essentially concerned with the vital preparation for the Harvest Time: the greatest spiritual opportunity for mankind in the world today.

The Sheep and the Goats

From *The Aquarian Gospel*
of Jesus the Christ

33 *Be ready at every moment of the day and night, because*
   when you expect him not the Lord will come.

34 *Behold, when he will come with all his messengers of light,*
   the Book of Life, and that of Records, shall be opened up —
   the books in which the thoughts and words and deeds are
   written down.

35 *And everyone can read the records he has written for himself, and he will know his doom before the judge shall speak,
and this will be the sifting time.*

36 *According to their records, men will find their own.*

37 *The judge is Righteousness, the king of all the Earth, and he
will separate the multitudes as shepherds separate the sheep
and goats.*

38 *The sheep will find their places on the right, the goats upon
the left, and every man will know his place.*

39 *And then the judge will say to those upon the right, "You
blessed of the Father-God, come unto your inheritance,
which was prepared for you from times of old.*

40 *"You have been servants of the race; I was hungry and you
gave me bread; was thirsty and you gave me drink; was
naked and you gave me clothes;*

41 *"Was sick, you ministered to me; was in prison and you
came to me with words of cheer; I was a stranger and in
your homes I found a home."*

42 *Then will the righteous say, "When did we see you hungry,
thirsty, sick, imprisoned or a stranger at our gates and ministered to you?"*

43 *And the judge will say, "You served the sons of men, and
whatsoever you have done for these, that you have done for
me."*

44 *The judge will say to those upon the left, "Depart from me;
you have not served the sons of men.*

45 *"I was hungry and you gave me naught to eat; was thirsty
and you gave me naught to drink; was a stranger and you
drove me from your door; I was imprisoned and was sick,
you did not minister to me."*

46 *Then these will say, "When did we thus neglect to care for
you? When did we see you hungry, thirsty, sick, a stranger
or in prison and did not minister to you?"*

47 *And then the judge will say, "Your life was full of self; you
served the self and not your fellow man, and when you
slighted one of these, you slighted and neglected me."*

48 *Then will the righteous have the kingdom and the power,
and they who are unrighteous shall go forth to pay their
debts, to suffer all that men have suffered at their hands.*

49 *They who have ears to hear and hearts to understand will
comprehend these parables.*

The Planetary Deadline

IF WE COULD LOOK DOWN FROM OUTER SPACE upon the earth with clairvoyant vision we would see the auric field of the planet as a murky ball of seething mist and fog. We might stand aghast at beholding this great dark cloud of subtle matter, which would evidence itself to be of a density and thickness that indicated not only impenetrability but also those conditions that are unfavorable to life and which make all things appear unclear and distorted. Thus it would be appreciated that there is a pressing need for change and global decontamination, for preparation by all those upon Earth who would be ready to weather well the approaching purificatory storm and, moreover, who would take advantage of it.

The effects of the cumulative and harmful thought-patterns and attitudes of humanity are pervasive worldwide, and are sorely evident today not only in the lives of mankind, but also upon the physical planet. Man has generally treated the Earth with gross disrespect for far too long. He has regarded his home together with its mineral, vegetable and animal kingdoms most carelessly, and has repeatedly demonstrated an attitude of negligence that expresses the erroneous view that the resources of the planet are for his own selfish use and exploitation alone. Humanity, as a whole, has completely overlooked the fact that Mother Earth—Gaia—is a spiritual being, engaged in her own evolutionary development, and who lovingly endeavours to provide a perfectly balanced environment for the peaceful and harmonious existence of multifarious lifeforms, including human beings.

The subject of impending Earth changes as a corollary of mankind's negligence and wrongdoing is a well-vented issue around the world today, and the geophysical aspects of the planetary events to come will not be detailed here. However, even though man has to some degree apparently understood the immediate crisis with which all life is faced upon the planet, he has clearly indicated that he is either unwilling or incapable of rectifying the extensive global damage that he himself has inflicted. So the pollution continues, and still the rape of planet Earth and the prostitution of her resources persist. The patient intelligence of Nature will only allow such abuse to continue up to a certain critical point, enduring man's violations for as long as possible in order that he may be given ample opportunity to learn from his mistakes and therefore change his ways of his own free will. Such is the great compassion of Mother Earth for her children.

In past, the unseen Guides of the race—the planetary Hierarchy—have recognized the necessity of standing by while the forces set up by man's own ignorance proceeded to react upon him, thus demonstrating the consequences of his thoughtlessness and foolish actions. In such compensating circumstances it was anticipated that man might readjust his life appropriately and change his ways of subsistence and leisure by ceasing to ravage and to pollute the Earth, and so save both his planet and himself from unnecessary and traumatic results. Thus humanity was given adequate occasion to discover that disengagement from selfishness, greed and materialism carries its own reward, and it was hoped that man would have liberated himself due to his education of suffering and, therefore, that he would have begun to live an intelligent life in harmony with natural law. To the contrary, however, mankind has demonstrated its extreme failure to react appropriately and positively to the warning signs given by Nature, and so today the human race and planet Earth are uncomfortably close to a red-alert condition.

A state of emergency has now arisen and we have arrived at both the need for a major turnaround in awareness and its intelligent application in the world, for we cannot continue along our selfish and unthinking lines of approach and survive much longer. There is an inordinate lack of good health, happiness, unity and peace in the world today, and the current gloomy planetary conditions are symptoms of extensive world ignorance. However, with the indispensable help that Servers are here to provide, such dismal prospects are shortly to change as the New World must and will be born.

The urgently needed process of global purification and healing which shall lead to eventual redemption for planet Earth is currently underway and is progressing mainly upon subtle planes. This vital activity is reconditioning and revitalizing the planet's auric field, and such inner changes necessarily precede and will ultimately affect the positive transformation of our physical world via its subtle energy grid system. This system consists of a meshwork of invisible forces that together form a kind of energy web that occupies space upon the inner planes that correspond to the physical body of the globe. The planetary grid performs a similar function for the Earth as do the subtle energy meridians within the human body, e.g., the regulation of balance (health), the distribution of vital life-forces, the relaying of impulses from one location to another (like nerves sending messages to the brain), etc. Wherever major lines of force intersect, perpendicular projections of whirling energy—or vortexes—emerge, each bearing its own unique properties. These comprise the *chakra* system of the Earth, and function—again like their human counterpart—as channels for the receipt and transmission of various energies from the unseen worlds. The planetary energy network as a whole is an extremely complex system; one that endeavours to maintain itself in a state of healthy balance. However, today it is in dire need of remedial attention, for disharmony and disease have there become prevalent and, as a result, are also manifesting everywhere in the physical world. Hence the ongoing work of repair and transmutation which is being effected by Servers who are labouring dutifully both upon the inner side of life as well as on the physical plane.

The bio-energetic network of every human being is inseparably linked to that of the planetary grid. Therefore, as our whole globe is purged and transformed, mankind is concurrently and similarly affected. All these important changes are being made in preparation for a great world transition that will culminate in the major release of powerful forces upon the planet and will mark the birth of the New World. This glorious event will represent a vital part of the Divine Plan for Earth in its current phase and will be experienced by all who successfully pass the forthcoming trials which necessarily precede such a momentous occasion.

Those divine Intelligences who are principally in charge of the regulation and distribution of karmic effects upon Earth are, in their great compassion, concerned for mankind in that it may be as prepared as possible to receive safely and beneficially the influx of light-energy that will be shortly introduced from the higher planes by way of the modified planetary grid and vortex system. In past, the influx of energies have been controlled and stepped down by these incorporeal Servers in accord with humanity's ability to receive the higher vibrational forces. Mankind has, therefore, been given sufficient opportunity to prepare in order to successfully integrate the corresponding transformations that these new frequencies necessitate. However, the global crisis today is so advanced, the Earth is in such a critical condition, and the planetary deadline is now so imminent that very soon the new energy grid will necessarily be activated, regardless of the proportion of humanity that is ready. Due to the present world crisis, further delay has become inexpedient. Mother Earth has entered the early stages of her labour, the moment of complete planetary alignment with a new density is now rapidly approaching; the New World is about to be born and every true soul will know its salvation.

The dedicated collaboration of a minimal number amongst humanity is required for the great shift to be achieved; yet due to the fact that in the past the number of souls required to constitute the critical mass could not be mustered, the planetary Hierarchy has been forced to make necessary postponements; humanity has not been ready to cooperate with its spiritual Elders for the important cause of its own liberation. To date, this is generally still the case, and so more and more Servers have been incarnating upon the physical plane during the last few decades in order to satisfy planetary karmic law by contributing toward the critical mass, thus accepting the same grand opportunity which the majority of human beings have thus far ignored. However, each day the planetary deadline draws closer and every person will soon find that they are coerced by the intensifying world conditions to brace themselves in preparation for the veritable tidal waves of divine force that are about to radically alter life on Earth. The frequency of the planetary vibration is presently escalating; everything in the world today is speeding up in readiness to receive the forthcoming torrents of vital energy, and this inevitable process has been prophetically termed 'The Quickening.'

Many Servers who are presently in incarnation have been preparing over numerous lifetimes for their impending final success and subsequent release from the grossness of the old Earth. For them the birth of the New World will signify the long-awaited fulfilment of a grand mission that began ages ago, while for a number of other 'younger' souls, it will throw open for the very first time the Portal of Initiation inviting them to cross the threshold dividing the physical plane from the higher worlds. This unparalleled opportunity for the ascension of consciousness will be expedited for many human beings as awakened Servers guide and accompany them into the New World in group formation, and in thus precipitating a much brighter awareness globally, the ensuing collective awakening of mankind will ultimately facilitate the prophesied return of the Christ-Consciousness upon Earth.

It is imperative that Servers awaken and take up their positions before the planetary deadline is reached, or face the grim prospect of failing their duty. The day of opportunity is with us—both for Servers and humanity—but it has its term. Today's unprecedented occasion, full of grace, is not forever lasting and will not dawn again for all those rejected souls for many thousands of years. The goals and purposes of the Divine Plan for this closing period of the Piscean age will come to an ultimate conclusion, and soon. The planetary time-clock will presently strike the hour, sounding the end of this cycle. At that moment, those who are ready to receive the descent of higher frequencies of spiritual energy will rise and prevail as they pass with the Earth into a more expansive dimension.

The Divine Plan for planet Earth cannot fail, for it is in line with the Great Scheme of Evolution designed by the One Creative Universal Intelligence; therefore it must and will go ahead. The Aquarian age will bring in a civilization, culture and fresh spirituality that will be utterly different to anything hitherto known. All those of humanity who, along with Servers, aspire to take their rightful place before the presently widening portal of opportunity that leads to the New World, should ensure today that they are informed, aware, dedicated and so prepared to confidently welcome the imminent planetary deadline and to consequently greet the New Dawn with a song of gratitude and joy.

Unity Consciousness

THE AQUARIAN AGE brings with it new and adjusted laws for the advanced spiritual progress of mankind, and these laws will do more than meet the requirements of today's expanding world consciousness. As the whole planet moves onto its next and highest turn of the evolutionary spiral, humanity is being exhorted by the new laws and by the divine Agents who implement them, to realize unity and true spiritual fellowship: a new and beautiful way of being. Such an ideal is not only possible in this concluding period of the Piscean era, but is also a prerequisite for the redemption and healing of both the Earth and mankind.

Success and survival into the New Age is a question of *us*, not I. All man-made policies, systems and businesses that have been built upon or which continue to be motivated by selfish values are today degenerating from within, and this process is destined to culminate in their complete demise. This is due to the fact that, in accord with the birth of the New World, all energies that have in past been successfully drawn upon by individuals or groups harbouring selfish motives are now being irreversibly withdrawn. Those who continue to live for self or who seek to make a living by working for organizations that exist solely to make personal profits, will experience growing tension, confusion and conflict in their lives as they become progressively devitalized and debilitated, and this will ultimately lead to mental, emotional and even physical illness. Conversely, the incoming energies of regeneration that constitute the new etheric blueprint for the construction of the New World may only be evoked by selfless, cooperative attitudes and activities. Such is one of the new laws of the Aquarian age.

In order that the new world paradigm of a united awareness may become a reality, it is necessary that ideas originating from the higher planes make an impact upon the consciousness of man, for the collective mind of humankind is the most important instrument through which the Divine Plan can manifest itself upon Earth. Consequently, mankind is being called to awaken in order that it may partake in the creation of the New World, and thus move forward spiritually as a race. Yet the immediate spiritual opportunity presented to humanity today is also perhaps its most difficult challenge, for success is greatly impeded by the seemingly impenetrable psycho-emotional smog that envelopes the planet, and which must be dissipated before new light may illuminate mankind's consciousness. This noxious *thought-cloud* was spawned eons ago by evil minds of extraterrestrial origin for their own premeditated and sinister purposes, and has been subsequently and continually fed by the negativity resulting from mankind's own blindness and ignorance; a blindness imposed by the long-controlling forces of materialism, and an ignorance bred into almost every child from birth and throughout their education in society during innumerable generations of mental and emotional constriction perpetrated by parents and teachers who themselves knew no better. The unhealthy global psychic atmosphere today is responsible worldwide for excessive disease and unnaturally short life-spans as it greatly hinders the well-being and natural evolution of all life that struggles within its oppressive influence.

The human race has proven itself to be incapable of self-rescue. Mankind, by itself, could never penetrate the world thought-cloud, and is today actually on a direct course to becoming entirely suffocated and destroyed by it. In reviewing esoteric history, we discover that past civilizations elsewhere in the cosmos managed to completely annihilate themselves together with their whole globe, and this was due to the inevitable outcome that ensues when a planet becomes entirely saturated with negative thought-currents. Rest assured, however, Mother Earth is not going to implode and disintegrate just yet! Humanity has clearly demonstrated its urgent need for help if the planet is to be salvaged, and that help is presently being given, for our world is a vital organ in the solar body* as well as a nexus of knowledge and information, and is therefore far too important to many other forms of life throughout our galaxy for its destruction to be allowed to occur. Aided, driven and sustained by irresistible divine forces that will appropriately eradicate all outmoded and stifling world standards in order to prepare the planet for its rebirth, interstellar Servers are presently intervening in humanity's ruinous course, for the Earth must be redeemed and healed before the New World can be born.

* * *

As has already been mentioned, an influx of incarnating Servers has been and is still growing today upon Earth in order to help pre-

---

*   Planet Earth is the *vishudda chakra* (throat centre) of the Deity (*Logos*) that is our solar system. When the Servers accomplish their collective task of 'clearing the throat' of the solar Logos, It's song shall once again, as in ancient times, harmonize with the celestial chorus of the Cosmos.

pare for the future, and to exemplify a new way of living. Unity consciousness is the new clarion keynote being sounded throughout the world by these emissaries, for they clearly recognize that selfless collaboration is vitally needed in order to liberate planet Earth, which is still presently permeated by a separative consciousness. They are well aware that only the potency of *synergetic union* as a collective force for Good upon Earth can dispel the accumulated darkness of ages past, overcome global fear, negativity and disease, and thus manifest the present world objective.

Servers are here today to deftly reveal to humanity that the only way to reverse its suicidal course toward disaster is by using Law against law, the Higher forces against the lower, effectively transmuting all that is obsolete and undesirable into that which is new and vital. This is accomplished by sowing contemporarily-relevant understanding where there is ignorance, by showing compassion where there is blame, in returning charity for greed and by giving love in exchange for enmity. It is by actually living in unity consciousness (i.e., with due awareness of and consideration for the collective whole) that Servers introduce a higher vibrational pattern within the Earth's auric field, and the new frequencies of spiritual light evoked by their positive activity today are contributing significantly toward the redemption of our planet and all life thereon. This they are qualified to do because all Servers have, prior to their individualization in Earthly incarnation, epitomized unity consciousness and, therefore, selfless service by their natural way of being; such is their attained level of evolution. For them, communal rapport and harmony is a customary life-configuration and has been so for a very long time. Thus so, they are adept at exemplifying group solidarity, and will again in this, their present incarnation upon Earth, demonstrate that cooperation, unity and love are among the greatest contributive factors for raising the planetary consciousness and thus effecting world healing.

In recent times, Servers have mainly incarnated as illumined individuals, and from this vantage point they have sought to help humanity in making further advances in its development, be it socially, politically, scientifically, spiritually, etc. Although to all appearances such pioneers may have seemed to be alone, as Servers they emanated from spheres of united souls, yet chose to incarnate individually in order to meet the requirements of and to better fit in with the consciousness of the period. Abraham Lincoln, Albert Einstein and Nikola Tesla are just some among a great host of Servers who have, over the centuries, incarnated specifically to assist in humanity's progress. Presently, however, in line with current needs and the general level of mankind's consciousness, large groups of exceptionally evolved Servers have incarnated into physical bodies having, prior to birth, temporarily relinquished many of their higher faculties and exalted consciousness in order that they may demonstrate to humanity interdependent and complementary group alliance. Their individual limitations in physical embodiment ensure that Servers will be drawn to work together in groups so that success in their collective mission may be known. Servers need one another, and at the time of their destined reunification upon Earth, they will manifest and exemplify unity consciousness: the New Way of conscious spiritual advancement for mankind in the Aquarian age.

There are other important motivations behind the Servers' sacrifice upon their current terrestrial assignment. Firstly, were they to reveal their full spiritual status to the world at this time, displaying their most elevated level of consciousness and exhibiting their unusual abilities, certain risks would be involved, for they would be in danger of living as an object of adulation by those amongst humanity who might be disposed to confer great praise upon them. For a Server to establish such a saintly reputation upon Earth, even unwittingly, would go against the specific design of the Divine Plan for this period, and would be most detrimental to its longer-term success. Exactly as all genuine spiritual teachers and leaders have done in the past, Servers have come to show the way by example. They do not wish to be worshipped, for to be thus idolized would be inappropriate for those who seek to inspire others to realize their own innate divinity, and to subsequently cooperate voluntarily with the divine Will for the planet.*

Secondly, it is in sharing and experiencing the conditions of mankind that empathy and compassion for the present human predicament is awakened. Servers come to Earth in order to demonstrate a vital and contemporary pattern for mankind; what all men and women must do, Servers must also do. Servers have incarnated as harbingers to exemplify the process of transformation which all

---

* Servers know that the period in which looking to and following gurus or individual spiritual leaders for guidance is now past, and that the greater intelligence that will precipitate in the Aquarian age will decree that unity consciousness be realized as a prerequisite for spiritual progress to be made in the New World.

who will enter the New World must undergo. A person cannot truly teach that which they do not demonstrate in their own life. By themselves undergoing the necessary process of post-natal forgetfulness, seeking, personal purification, spiritual discovery, remembrance and initiation into the New World Consciousness (which is unity consciousness), and by thus exemplifying the Way, Servers construct a path from the old to the New, preparing and making easier the road for those who choose to follow. They act as a bridge between the spiritual worlds and the world of material form, and they create a very wide bridge indeed when they unite and work as one in their particular soul group. This they do in order to inspire others to take advantage of the greatest opportunity ever known in human history upon Earth, and to thereby help mankind to convert current world potential into a splendid reality.

* * *

In conformity with the nature of their voluntary service, today's Servers undergo an intricate method of incarnation which differs significantly from that of ordinary individual souls. Once the necessary calculations have been made in accord with the overall design of the Divine Plan, families of souls—or group-souls—decide when and where on Earth to take their incarnation, and they begin their descent toward the denser spheres of our planet, maintaining for the present time group cohesiveness. The division of a group-soul ensues partly at the time of physical conception and progresses during the maturation of the foetus and following birth as the child matures. Thereafter, throughout a variable time period of terrestrial life and as the planetary deadline approaches, the group-soul continually projects more of itself down into each individual manifestation as its various personalities develop their physical, emotional and mental faculties. This process could be compared to a gas burner with numerous jets. As the gas is slowly turned up, the light of each seemingly individual flame becomes brighter, yet all the flames have a common source. If, in the mind's eye, the gas burner is inverted so that the source (symbolizing the higher planes) is above the flames (representing the lower spheres including the physical plane), a simplistic but accurate image of this rather abstruse procedure of group-soul incarnation may be acquired.

It may be seen, then, that the consciousness of the *real* Server is a great deal more expansive than that which he is able to demonstrate as an individual in the waking state on the physical plane (and even in his spiritually awakened state). Only a very small part of the Server's full expression can ever be reproduced in the comparatively coarse physical matter of the human body, the physical brain and nervous system being able to manifest but a fraction of the far greater entity—the group-soul—which is chiefly resident in its own world, and the Server's personality is but an outpost for a far greater intelligence. In truth, Servers taking physical incarnation have never really left home, but have only sent tiny fragments of themselves down through the denser vehicles of expression that exist in the lower worlds: mental, emotional and physical. Servers have taken embodiment upon Earth in order to render their service upon all of these lower planes, although to the limited third-density consciousness of the ordinary person it will appear that only the physical plane is influenced. However, this is only a part of the Servers' total service, as any good clairvoyant will testify.

The temporarily-separated lives (or fragmented representatives of the group-soul) attempt to take incarnation within a reasonably short time of others that have been assigned to the same group task in order that, as individual personalities, they may ultimately reunite upon the physical plane to work together toward certain group ends.* These committed groups of Servers incarnate life after life and pass through similar preparatory experiences in readiness for the final consummation of their extended collective work. Bonds of kinship forged between group-souls (incarnating as multiple personalities) over many lifetimes may thus become knit so strongly that they will be incapable of misunderstanding or mistrusting one another when the trials of the greater work which they are destined to do come upon them in the future. The one important fact that the reunited individuals are devoted in service to the Divine Plan overpowers all other considerations, and the group is thus magnetized together in order that it may perform that service upon Earth as one focussed and united body.

The reunification upon the physical plane of the personalities

---

* There are various permutations of this manner and order of group-soul incarnation that span the millennia and may encompass many different planets and densities as integral parts of the overall group task. However, the method here described represents a general trend, and one that is particularly applicable during this present and culminating phase of the Servers' collective mission upon Earth.

belonging to the group-soul facilitates the restoration of a united consciousness that is so complete and so perfect that individuals do not see one another simply as close friends, or even as spiritual brothers and sisters, but as aspects of one multifaceted entity, one service-mind. Due to their collective alignment with the Law of Love and intelligent Purpose, each individual Server consciously cooperates with all the others in the group for the benefit of the world. Living in and for Truth and righteousness, all members abide in absolute openness, unconditioned by the usual Earthly environment of fear, distrust and self-absorption, and they express themselves from a place of unhindered spiritual contact, which naturally impels their dedication to the group good as well as humanity's spiritual progress. Such group at-one-ment (wherein lies the secret of telepathy) creates a strong and stable platform from which each person or group within the community can serve at their own preferred level and expression, thus retaining their individuality while simultaneously able to tap the collective wellspring of love, knowledge and spiritual vitality that supports and strengthens each member in their chosen line of service.

As Servers join together once again in what is for them a familiar spirit of united purpose, they naturally begin to invoke powerful forces for the blessing of the world, and so demonstrate something of the great spiritual potential that is available today to all unified groups that choose to serve the Divine Plan. Awakened Servers, when in focussed group formation, have the ability to channel the prayers of mankind through the *group heart* and up toward divine spheres. The invocational potency of light and grace working under the directives of a group consciousness is enormously greater than that which may be known individually. Two thousand years ago, Christ, through Jesus, expounded this vital esoteric principle, which is especially pertinent in the Aquarian age. He averred that: *"When two or more people come together in my name, I shall be there with them."* This symbolic phrase refers to the Law of Synergy, which may be evoked *when two or more people* unite for the collective good, or *in my name*, i.e., in the name of Christ, or divine Love. This law, in being implemented by dedicated groups, will ultimately be responsible for attracting to Earth certain holy forces that will, in turn, precipitate Christ-Consciousness in some, while simultaneously attracting the attention and cooperation of certain exalted incorporeal beings who themselves naturally express the Christed frequency (which is a united field of awareness), hence *I shall be there with them*. This now impending grand evocation of Divinity upon Earth has come to be known by Christians as "The Coming Again of Christ," and awakened Servers may contribute toward its unfoldment naturally and with ease due to their unselfish attitudes and close association with the multifarious spiritual Hierarchies who reside and work from within the hidden worlds and who are assisting with the planetary transformations.

The advantages of a united or group consciousness working as one unit for the receipt and transmission of divine forces are legion and extremely powerful. The principle of synergy, which is only applicable in group work, shall contribute toward rapid global awakening like never before upon Earth, as the process of radiating the Christ-Consciousness unfolds worldwide. Once mankind observes the far-reaching significance of selfless cooperation and divine fellowship, the advantages of utilizing the complementary virtues of individual group members for the greater whole will be actualized all over the world, and consequently a brighter, more expansive light of a new and harmonious way of living will dawn within the minds and hearts of humanity. It is at this time that the secret of the Law of Synthesis will be restored within humanity's consciousness (having been mercifully withdrawn in Atlantean times), and only then will the world's problems be resolved as the natural planetary rhythm is stabilized and elevated to a new order. Such is the magnitude and import of the task belonging to present-day Servers who will exemplify the new spiritual standards for the Aquarian age and so lay the foundations for the next step to be taken by mankind.

* * *

Particularly in light of the present unbalanced world condition, it should not be expected that the release of tremendous divine force upon the planet in the near future will fail to have its corresponding tumultuous side effects. The coming upheavals will greatly affect all societies worldwide, and as the old methods of livelihood decline toward eventual collapse during the approaching years, those with foresight will pull together in order to support one another throughout the transition period. Their clear vision of the future will reveal to them that a gradual and calculated renunciation of everything of the old will prepare them in stages for the necessary, final and complete abandonment of past social and political systems in exchange for that which is new and better.

Many and diverse groups are presently working to facilitate the entry of very new ideals and aims into the consciousness of the human race. The great efforts underway are perfectly in accord with human potential, and the final goal is assured of success. As the vital energies of the new cycle are streaming into the Earth's energy grid, extraordinary opportunities for group accomplishment are being created. Genuine selfless collaboration evokes help from the hidden side of life, and the work that various groups around the world are today effecting is hastening the all important process of raising the planetary vibration, while simultaneously helping to alleviate the inevitable distress and disorder that will ensue as the global transformations proceed. Nothing in the world can resist the cumulative enthusiasm of a number of sincere and dedicated people working together in an organized group for a common and selfless cause, for such truly spiritual activity is one with the Universal Activity. Some groups are today releasing that there are sure esoteric methods whereby they can manifest anything they need for the collective good. Unity consciousness is the key, and when groups of committed people can love enough they are able to draw energy from the higher worlds which can manifest eventually upon the physical plane in whatever form is required to further their work.

Motivations based upon a shared and true vision of future world-unification are impelling Servers today to unite as members of the New Societal Fellowships. They are becoming inspired to move toward wholehearted cooperation with all those incarnated souls who comprehend something of the Divine Plan, and who are ready to dedicate their lives and all their resources to the One Great Work upon Earth. A growing proportion of mankind is now taking the necessary steps forward to improve the present world condition by expanding its vision to embrace the greater whole. The objective of the Divine Plan for Earth is, therefore, being currently expedited as humanity itself comes to appreciate the situation with which it is immediately faced.

Servers offer others the chance to rise up like a phoenix from the ashes of past ignorance and to join together in active cooperation and preparation for what lies ahead, yet awakened Servers will never impose upon the free will of others. They undertake only to inspire and encourage humanity to make an intelligent choice to unite for world service by recognizing the demands of the hour and by achieving alignment with the new and adjusted laws of the Aquarian age through the active application of love and wisdom in daily life. Assisting Servers in their duties and giving to them in charity for the One Divine Work of sublimating the planetary consciousness will result in the generation of beneficent karmic merit; serving with them will avail the altruist of the greatest spiritual opportunity offered upon Earth today. Those members of the race who are uniting with Servers at this time are already aligning themselves with the present unique spiritual opportunity. Those who do not take advantage of such benefits may still learn at a later time, although stragglers may find themselves painfully forced into the only sane option in these times once the great storm begins to rage.

Important considerations must be made, however, when preparing for genuine, spiritual group work. It should be remembered that since everything in the universe is interconnected, each thought, feeling and activity evokes a response from the subtle energies of the various planes. Each member—depending upon their own auric condition and in affecting the whole—either hinders or aids the group. A chain is as strong as its weakest link, and the united auras of group members ever determine the group's limitation or success. Hence emerges various issues. Among them: each individual's responsibility to the group, one's attitudes and motivations, and most importantly the informed and, therefore, intelligent dedication of every member of the working unit to serving the Divine Plan for planet Earth.

Mental and emotional handicaps such as fear, pride, selfishness, etc., even if maintained upon subconscious levels, will hold the group vibration down, reduce the group's radiatory field and attract like energies to the intended work, thus restricting the potential of the group's positive spiritual effect. Mixed motivations yield variables that may easily prevent a positive synergy. If members are thinking of themselves in any way; if they possess personal vanity, such as might show itself in the desire to shine or to take a prominent part in the proceedings; if they have any selfish motivations for joining the group, however subtle, or if they have not wholly and selflessly consecrated themselves to the Work of Christ, then they constitute a weak link. Such individuals must grasp the fact that they join, not to receive, but to give; not to be interested and amused, but to take their share in a great Work for the good of the planetary life. A genuine love of that life and of humanity is the one credential that will qualify affiliation within the ranks of Servers, nothing less.

Earnest and benevolent collaboration is today establishing a new and much needed spiritual foundation in the world—a living model of true fellowship—that will encourage humanity in the Aquarian age to tread the path together, helping one another toward the realization of a life of balance, rapport and unity. The life-pattern and expression of communities in the new era may be analogously compared to healthy brain cells working symbiotically as one greater and singularly-focussed creative mind. Such communities will exemplify that union is harmony and strength, and that well-regulated and simultaneous efforts always produce wonders. This has been the secret of all successful associations, communities and civilizations throughout history. The astonishing accomplishments achieved by ant and bee colonies may be regarded as an example of the very real possibilities that may be actualized by a one-pointed group mind. The question may arise, however: can we, or should we, really model our lives upon the crude examples given by insects!? Well, why not? *"As above, so below,"* and, therefore, as below, so above! Ants and bees have been exemplifying a vital universal principle to mankind for millions of years, ever since the planetary Hierarchy first arrived upon Earth. Together with wheat, ants and bees were introduced to our world by these spiritual luminaries, and it may be prudent to consider that such enlightened beings would certainly act for definite reasons. Today it is time to take heed of those examples that were left for mankind ages ago.

An important part of the Servers' function on Earth at this time—the instigation and spread of unity consciousness—will be accomplished through the establishment of the New Societal Fellowships, and it is through them that a congenial environment for the advent of the New World Consciousness will be fostered. Such colonies will reflect the structure and collective functional mode of all the great spiritual Hierarchies that exist throughout the universe, and they will contain the seeds for the future efflorescence of living super-social entities that are destined to flourish upon Earth subsequent to the birth of the New World. These spiritual societies will enable the sustained physical incarnation of members of the local planetary Hierarchy in the future, and so help to perpetuate true spiritual fellowship upon Earth. Unity consciousness may be rightfully seen, therefore, as an integral part of an ineffably vast and magnificent blueprint conceived within the Universal Mind long ago. This Plan is now beginning to be appreciated and applied by mankind upon the physical plane again, just as it has been successfully by various old and even ancient civilizations of the past, only at the close of the present major cycle the whole world will join together in the sweetest hymn ever sung upon Earth: a divine anthem of international cooperation, global goodwill and united spiritual purpose.

* * *

When each Server, through individual experience, has learned and synthesized the lessons assigned to their own personal mission, they will be ready to effect their specialized facet of service in unison with the group work. Such individual contributions are integral constituents of the One World Service, and also of the much larger overall Cosmic Task that ultimately employs countless legions of Servers within the various great Confederations of Helpers in service to the Divine Plan throughout the universe. The work of Servers upon Earth, then, may be regarded in its truest perspective as just a tiny holographic aspect of a vast intergalactic operation of universal government, which necessarily functions under the auspices of a united awareness.

The long-awaited moment of humanity's collective initiation into spiritual adulthood is nigh, and many human beings will soon become consciously aware of interstellar familial affiliations that predate the most ancient scriptures upon Earth today. In instigating a vital process of light-energy invocation for the world, selfless group alliance will serve to bridge the existing gulf between mankind and these civilizations, which constitute the greater part of its cosmic family. For the very first time since the original 'creator-gods' walked amongst men on Earth eons ago, the human race will know and claim its heritage as worthy members of a trans-galactic society spanning a multitude of worlds and densities throughout Infinity. This momentous reunification of long-separated celestial families will help bring about the initiation of Mother Gaia herself—anticipated for millions of years—as she fulfils a major part of her own spiritual destiny and becomes again universally recognized as the jewel of the solar system; one very small but nevertheless important globe amongst a vast network of stellar systems extending in all directions, pervading the Cosmos, and which have been actively functioning as intelligent, living satellites of the divine Will for long ages.

Humanity's destiny is already inscribed within the ancient pages of the Divine Plan, and thus it is known that all those servants of the race who are today working toward establishing a united awareness upon Earth will demonstrate how to live consciously as one creative intelligence, coalescing in accord with the universal Law of Unity. As precursors of the New World Consciousness, awakened Servers thus personify the forthcoming Divinity in manifestation upon Earth. Illuminating a clear path by venturing dauntlessly ahead, bearing the revealing light of unity consciousness like a polestar offering sure guidance forward, Servers blaze a safe passage through the shadowy realms of confusion and erroneous thinking, and so lead the way confidently in group formation from past selfishness, separation and misery into the liberating resplendence of the Golden Age of Aquarius.

Inherent Characteristics of Servers

NOW THAT A GENERAL OUTLINE of the servers' origins, motivations and collective purpose upon Earth has been ascertained, we may venture forth to explore in greater detail their unique characteristics, qualities, challenges, opportunities and other associated phenomena.

In order to really be in service to the Divine Plan, a person's sympathetic understanding and regard for the Greater Life must have transcended their preoccupation with personal issues to a degree where they are naturally able to align their ideals, thoughts, actions and their life's purpose with a higher cause than that of their own progress and welfare. Essentially, a Server may be defined as any earnest individual who attempts to live a righteous life, and who, therefore, abides in unselfish service and dedication to the greatest good of which they have become aware. They may be distinguished by their natural tendencies to selflessly seek the Truth, and by their inherent and genuine desire to be of some spiritual help to their fellows. Anyone, therefore, at any time may qualify to join the ranks of the Servers, from whatever cosmic origins they may spring, and regardless of what they may have done in the past. The mark of a real servant of life is their present purity of motive, sincerity and unconditionally loving attitude.

However, we are here principally concerned with those Servers who have voluntarily incarnated upon this planet in order to contribute specifically toward furthering the Divine Plan for Earth in its present phase. These strategically-incarnating souls may be classified together as a distinctive group to which certain unique and identifying attributes apply, often even from their early childhood. Such characteristics are numerous indeed; some of them are quite subtle and cannot be fully comprehended by the intellect. However, in order to help the reader to conclude for themselves whether they may belong to a group of Servers, some of their idiosyncrasies are here summarized.

1. A distinguishing mark of Servers in physical embodiment upon Earth is that at some time during their lives they will find that they possess a genuine, urgent and growing sense that they have some important duty to perform and that they are here to help, even if the details of their vaguely-remembered task remain unclear. They may be prompted from within to begin a search in the world for answers to certain naturally-arising questions which,

once resolved, may lead them onto the succeeding question and the next stage of their necessary quest to understand and to remember who they are.

Many Servers are today recalling an inner soul-memory that hints at the fact that they were once a member of a larger group of souls who, at some time prior to their present incarnation, collaborated together for a worthy cause. The Server's natural impulse to investigate the meaning of these particular inner senses is actually a reminder from within that they might do well to begin seeking both the purpose of their incarnation as well as members of their soul-group who are also currently in embodiment upon the physical plane. Inevitably, all Servers must eventually embark upon the path of seeking in order to prepare themselves to resume what is for them a familiar work upon this present and highest turn of the evolutionary spiral for planet Earth.

2. Servers incarnating from higher, more rarefied spheres than those of Earth (especially for the first time) will have become most accustomed to a much more pure and refined environment. Therefore, they may experience certain congenital difficulties in dealing with and adapting to third-density realities upon this planet. Servers generally have a sense, however dim, that the great travesty of the divine nature of life that is pervasively demonstrated here on Earth is not only undesirable, but is also entirely unnecessary. They perceive on some level that the gross distortion of Truth and the resultant suffering that is everywhere apparent is certainly not normal within the peaceful realms which they feel to be their true home, and to which, not surprisingly, they so often yearn to return.

However, Servers will generally find that they are propelled in two directions at once. While an irresistible magnetic pull draws them forward, onward and upward, ever seeking to avail them of that emancipation from suffering which they have known before, yet in moments of poignant recall of their ancient promise to humanity and planet Earth they are simultaneously compelled to turn away from the spiritual Sun in order to reach out and to share its light with the world.

Awakening Servers will at some stage recall living in other physical loci or within more subtle worlds where harmonious rapport with all beings, telepathic openness, spiritual fellowship and spontaneous, unbridled loving are the natural conditions of life. They often, therefore, bear some form of affliction which is due to their reaction to the Earth's psychic climate, and this may manifest in various ways. Personality disorders born of estrangement in a hostile world, physical ailments such as allergies, insomnia and hypersensitivity are just a few symptoms of the typical Server's malaise, and are indications of difficulties in adjusting to a far more dense and antagonistic environment than that of their native density. These problems may provoke certain individuals to turn toward such 'sedative measures' as alcohol, drugs, excessive eating, etc. in order to alleviate the depression of their homesickness.

Increasingly today Servers are experiencing various symptoms of the unfolding planetary cleansing.* Their subtle energy fields (auras) are presently undergoing refinement and expansion in order to receive the finer energies that are being released from the higher worlds. However, due to their rising sensitivity, Servers may also become affected (and infected) by the etheric effluvia that is such a widespread problem upon our detoxifying planet. In fact, awakening Servers generally reflect and express symptoms of the planet's purging process before the rest of mankind. As Earth frequencies rise, Servers are becoming particularly sensitive to psychic influences of all kinds; they will find that they are easily influenced by the thoughts and feelings of those around them. As tensions and impurities arise within the minds and emotions of humanity in accord with the scheduled and necessary purification of the Earth, the auras of most individuals are prone to become inflamed, as it were, and are much more inclined to impinge detrimentally upon the auras and, therefore, the consciousness of others. This often causes much stress for Servers, for example, in the form of anxiety, paranoia, depression, neurosis and even psychosis, and may at worst lead eventually to some kind of physical infirmity. Indeed, such are common afflictions experienced by anyone who is susceptible to the auric encroachment from adverse vibratory influences that abound today in an ailing world.

Apprehension, fear and nervous agitation are presently escalating in the world as the polarities of good and evil, Truth and falsehood are being magnified in accord with the inflowing frequencies of Aquarian energy, and this is a normal pattern on Earth at the close of a major cycle. Auric bombardment is especially intensified in cities and other highly populated areas for obvious reasons. Additionally, as sensitivity heightens for all humanity in accord

---

* This currently ongoing process, which has been much prophesied throughout the ages and up to date, is described in detail in a volume entitled *The New Call*, and is available upon request. (See end of document).

with the unfolding world changes, toxic emanations such as harmful electromagnetic frequencies, air and noise pollution, unnatural and noxious additives in foodstuffs, etc. will tend to cause progressively greater adversity for the reactive majority. One's environment necessarily affects one's consciousness, and this is decidedly and profoundly so for awakening Servers. However, should the pertinent occult dynamics of such phenomena be understood well, and should one's life be adjusted accordingly, then negative reactions may be minimized and largely avoided. There is a very effective way to rise above all the adverse conditions that will be known by virtually everyone in the immediate future, a solution that is surprisingly simple indeed and which is herein discussed in detail.

It may seem quite ironic that while sensitivity is almost always troublesome for Servers in the earlier stages, it is actually beneficial to their overall task. This is because it allows them to procure a first-hand empathic comprehension of the crisis in which humanity is presently immersed. Therefore, an opportunity to discover and so pioneer new ways to effectively overcome today's unique and challenging circumstances is provided. Insight into how best to serve mankind is gained from personal experience, and this is a part of the duty that all Servers have accepted in order to assist in the important and necessary transformations upon planet Earth.

3. As natural psychic empaths, then, Servers readily and often unconsciously absorb the surrounding energies of their environment. As previously stated, such inherent sensitivity may sometimes result in rather chronic conditions for the Server at large, and those with a more fragile disposition who find themselves living and working in more densely-populated areas may at times become quite overwhelmed as they take on the negative psycho-emotional vibrations of those around them. However, this phenomenon represents only the first stage of a potential and critically important transmutation process of which all Servers are intrinsically capable whereby gross energies may be purified through them.

Awakening Servers are, by nature, *energy transmuters*, and this function is a very significant part of their overall task upon Earth. However, in identifying their own personality with the character of those energies around them which they so easily soak up, Servers who have not yet fully restored their higher awareness often allow themselves to lapse into the undesirable conditions that are triggered by local negative influences. In order to remain themselves untainted by deleterious external vibrations, while simultaneously performing their duty of transmutation for the world, Servers must recall their innate ability to sublimate gross energies. Such vital remembrance will be established once again only by awakening their natural and active disposition toward a selfless concern for the well-being of others. Love—never fear or selfish orientation—is the key to spiritual success for Servers (as well, of course, as humanity).

It is an immutable universal law that in dedicated and unselfish service, the vibratory rate of consciousness is raised. Like attracts like, and so the sincere, benevolent and active Servers will discover that they are able to rise above most exterior harmful vibrations, subsisting happily almost as if these energies did not exist at all. Protected by the positive orientation of a truly loving attitude, nothing of the grosser side of life can affect them, and they remain free to render that effective service to humanity for which they incarnated.

Servers who have reattained their ability to transmute energies may sometimes suddenly and unexpectedly manifest psycho-emotional states that are not at all related to their own present condition or past experiences. They would do well to understand the dynamic of this process of absorption and transmutation of the auric impurities of others, which is actually quite harmless and may even be a joyful experience if done correctly with spiritual understanding, detached compassion and righteous dedication to helping the world.

4. The aforementioned circumstances with which awakening Servers are confronted during the early stages of their unfolding mission will impel them toward adopting a loving yet ever dispassionate concern for the spiritual well-being of others. Consequently, and due to their necessary detachment and broader vision, Servers are frequently misunderstood, for the love which they express differs widely from the sentimental, affectionate and personal interest of the average person. They are necessarily occupied mainly with the spiritual prosperity of all humanity as a race, as well, of course, as all life. They are not primarily concerned with the petty interests of individuals who are predominantly occupied with their own little problems and concerns. Such impersonality regularly brings Servers under the criticism of others, and with this they must learn to live, and to it they need pay no attention. True, unconditional love for all is of far greater importance upon the journey of life than are personal relationships, yet while living in a world of desirous, reactive egos, Servers may find that they possess very few true friends. However, they will always know who their real friends are,

for genuine Servers of the Divine Plan will stand as One in group formation, looking out (of the personal) and upwards in the same direction.

Today, it is still not generally understood how love sees with perfect clarity the deficiencies of any form or expression—human or otherwise—and how it then proceeds to bend every effort toward aiding the indwelling life—the soul—to liberate it from the trammels of self-deception. Love wisely recognizes those who require guidance, and why; it hears with precision, perceiving that which resides within the heart of a person, and it ever seeks to unite and cooperate with all those truly compassionate members of humanity in the world for a meaningful cause. This it achieves not by blindness born of euphemistic politeness or personality sensitivities, but by discrimination and wisdom. Such is perfect love, which must include wisdom, and which is ever purposeful and intelligent as it strives to do what is best with regard always for the greatest spiritual good of all. To date, much emphasis has been laid upon that which is interpreted by most as 'love,' and not enough has been placed upon *wisdom*, which is *love expressing itself in service*. In order to be effective today, such service must recognize universal law, the significance of the period in which we live, and its adjusted and contemporary requirements for success during the times ahead.

Servers have already attained the spiritual goal of unconditional love and spontaneity of service prior to their present-day incarnation, and it is this achievement that has earned them the right and privilege to embark upon their assignment on Earth. However, due to the necessarily-imposed forgetfulness of their current human expression, it is the restoration and, therefore, present embodiment of the virtue of perfect love to which all awakening Servers today again aspire, whether they are consciously aware of it yet or not. The quest for the Holy Grail is again on worldwide, and its reward represents a magnificent trophy for every Server who would remember the sacred purpose of their incarnation.

Something of the prime spiritual impulse that guides the Servers' motives should here be understood. They will almost always offer others the choice to serve with them, to raise their own vibratory rate of consciousness, and so qualify for entrance into the New World. However, still today very few people in the world realize that real spiritual service is often destructive. This is necessarily so because old attachments, erroneous belief systems and false securities must be effaced in order that the light of the new and the true may illuminate the awareness. Those who are waiting to recognize their own preconditioned idea of the ideal and perfect spiritual teacher—as exemplified perhaps by the serene and graceful saints of past religions and biographies—are likely to miss the opportunities offered by the typical and necessarily more assiduous and demanding Server who is compelled to meet the planetary deadline having contributed to as large a harvest as possible.

Awakened Servers act as catalysts in relationships, and interaction with them is often dynamic, explosive and evocative of either the best or the worst in people. Due to their natural and purposeful disposition to focus steadfastly upon essentials and to get straight to the root of relevant issues, Servers often swiftly elicit in others that which needs to be recognized, addressed and resolved in order that the greatest spiritual opportunity may be taken by them at the forthcoming Harvest Time. However, in a world that predominantly demonstrates attitudes of fear, selfishness and resistance to change, the general reception with which Servers must learn to cope is often far from sympathetic, and sometimes even blatantly hostile. Although a great many people may *speak* of charity and selfless service, when given the opportunity to intelligently demonstrate these virtues, most fail to live up to their own ideals.

Whatever the response to their earnest endeavours, awakening Servers will always find the inspiration to continue to effect their duty to humanity by offering the truth of the times, however extraordinary or unbelievable that truth may appear to some. Indeed, the most valuable service that may generally be effected in the world by anyone today is to spread abroad factual information regarding the impending choice that every human being must make in these times, bearing in mind always that free will is a divine provision, and that individual choice must be honoured. By thus offering others the opportunity to respond positively, Servers provide mankind with important 'tests' during these "end times."

It is a lamentable fact, however, that the majority of human beings have become so blinded, sceptical and fearful during their Earthly experience that they all too often reject the spiritual succor offered them by other loving hearts who may approach them with open arms. Such widespread rejection of genuine concern and benevolence is often difficult for awakening Servers to fully comprehend, and they are regularly coerced to accept such circumstances even as recognized potential fades to futility before their eyes. The poet, Kahlil Gibran, experienced his own fair share of such treatment which he expresses succinctly in the following words: *"If I extend an empty hand and in retrieving it and finding it still empty, I feel disappointment, that is foolishness; yet if I extend a hand which is full and yet find no one to receive, then that is hopelessness."*

William Blake understood this element of human character also:

Children of the future Age,
Reading this indignant page,
Know that in a former time,
Love! Sweet Love! was thought a crime.

It is customary still upon this planet that when secular people hear a holy truth, they break into loud laughter. On Earth, perhaps if it were not laughable, it would not be a holy truth! Worldly and self-assured people may appear shrewd and clever, while a meek and humble servant of the race may seem to them to be quite foolish. Servers often learn hard but useful lessons through ridicule, rejection, and even by dint of the unwarranted hostility of others, yet courtesy of such a difficult education they will eventually come to the realization that intelligent reticence, silent compassion and loving thoughts frequently constitute the greatest service that they may render under certain circumstances.

A passage from the Hermetic Tradition in the *Kybalion* testifies to the dilemma which many Servers face during the earlier stages of their reawakening process:

> But a moment's glance back over the pages of history will show the wisdom of the Masters, who knew the folly of attempting to teach to the world that which it was neither ready or willing to receive. The Hermetists have never sought to be martyrs, and have, instead, sat silently aside with a pitying smile on their closed lips, while the 'heathens raged noisily about them' in their customary amusement of putting to death and torture the honest but misguided enthusiasts who imagined that they could force upon a race of barbarians the truth capable of being understood only by the elect who had advanced along the Path; and the spirit of persecution has not as yet died out in the land. There are certain Hermetic teachings which, if publicly promulgated, would bring down upon the teachers a great cry of scorn and revilement from the multitude, who would again raise the cry of "Crucify! Crucify!"

Servers, however, have certainly not incarnated in order to dwell in solitude like the Hermetists of old, nor indeed have they come from so far abroad merely to attain greater self-realization and mystical ecstasy for themselves alone, like a meditating yogi.

In the early stages and before the planetary deadline, awakening Servers constantly live the dual life of seemingly mundane yet serviceful activity, and of intense and simultaneous spiritual seeking, reflection and inner work. This is, in fact, one outstanding characteristic of the true spiritual aspirant of today in contradistinction to the aspirant of the past who typically escaped from life into the silent places and away from the pressures of daily living and constant contact with others. The task of the aspirant in the New World—exemplified today by all awakened Servers—is much more difficult than that of the monk or meditating hermit of the past, but their achievements and rewards will be still greater. This is to be expected as an integral part of world progress, and those Servers who in past centuries excelled in self-realization, mysticism, transcendentalism and the like are back again today as compassionate servants of the race, happily embracing the more advanced principles and laws that pertain to spiritual service and higher occultism.

The Latin word 'Occultus' means hidden. The occult, then, is the science of that which is hidden from the five physical sense-organs and the intellect. The previous reference to occultism (and the context in which the word is used throughout this book) signifies the attainment of an intelligent understanding of universal laws and esoteric principles, and, driven by unselfish motive, a conscious wielding of the hidden forces of Nature for the good of the whole. It does not imply sorcery, black magic, lower psychism, common mediumship, etc. It is difficult for those who know nothing of the occult to realize how great, how serious and how all-pervading are their own limitations.* The understanding of awakened Servers regarding the inner life and the occult dynamics of the Universe is generally much broader than that which humanity has in past possessed, and Servers will naturally, therefore, carry a much brighter

---

* Limitation and failure are always self-imposed, and the degree of success and the rapidity of awakening for each individual is, today as always, strictly self-determined, and may be expedited only by right attitude, right understanding, right choice and subsequent right action. Spiritual progress and its accompanying expansions of consciousness have ever been available to mankind, and are especially so at this time—the dawning of the Aquarian age—but only if and when the candidate has prepared adequately to receive this grace. Each person's fate is utterly dependent upon the use of his own free will.

lamp of truth and wisdom into the New World, illuminating the road ahead for everyone to see.

5. Those Servers who have today begun the search for understanding and so initiated their own reawakening process will witness that they are having curious effects upon some of the people with whom they come into contact. This is due to the faster vibratory energies which they attract and radiate by their earnest and spiritually-inquisitive attitudes. As they make their impact upon others, such energies may not always seem to produce favorable results, yet upon a closer and discerning inspection, the surfacing of emotional and psychological impurities may be recognized as both necessary and desirable if auric cleansing, healing and consequent preparation for harvest is to ensue.

Awakened Servers generally possess what might be termed *reflective auras*. This means that without effort and simply by being natural, they may perform a kind of *mirroring* function that allows others to become aware of their own psycho-emotional encumbrances. Awakened Servers are entirely free from the desire for personal acknowledgement, reward or the need to impress or control others. Therefore, they do not play into the ego-dramas of those who may themselves habitually enact them. This produces a mirroring effect because by not responding in the usual ways of the personality, and in therefore refraining from feeding and so encouraging the illusions of the separated ego, the latter may see itself, just as if it were looking upon the smooth surface of a perfectly still and reflective body of water. Where there is a lack of reactive validation to the expressions of the deluded ego, and where no identification is made with the volatile personality, the mirroring effect will almost always be experienced by the individual who is seeking such a response. In thus being thrown back on itself, the ego sees its reflection, and this can be a rather unsettling experience for most. Generally, people understand that if they can see themselves so clearly, then so can others, yet most often it is the case that the self-deceiving ego becomes most uncomfortable at having its illusions challenged by the mirror and thus its faults and weaknesses exposed, even in the presence of perfect acceptance and unconditional love, and the most common reaction of the typically embarrassed person in such a situation is blame, denial or both.

And this is not all. The energy fields that compose the subtle bodies of all awakening Servers also have a definite purging effect upon the auras of others, and should there exist a lack of understanding or restraint in some of those with whom Servers come into direct contact, this quality is bound to arouse certain negative reactions from unstable and unprepared egos. Reactions to purification may at worst erupt into irrational antagonism directed toward the Server, either silently in thought and feeling or blatantly by outward expression.

Although on a far lesser scale, the unavoidable persecutions of Servers may be rightfully compared to the crucifixion of Jesus, the Piscean Christ, as well as the executions of the martyrs whose lives lucidly evinced the inevitable result upon planet Earth when the darkness of ignorance is confronted by the light of Truth. As stipulated in all the greatest spiritual teachings, however, one's mood and state of consciousness are solely one's own responsibility. While the cowardly and ignorant readily point the finger of blame and condemnation at others, seeking to avoid, deny or change what *is*, the wise man quietly looks within himself for the root cause of his own reactions to external triggers, knowing that each and every one of life's circumstances provide valuable experience, opportunity to make prudent choices, and therefore ripe occasion for spiritual progress. As the planetary deadline moves ever closer, however, and as life on Earth becomes progressively more intense for everyone, violent catharsis will become a common reaction around certain awakening individuals and groups, and the more advanced among Servers shall witness their instrumentality in the necessary task of exorcising discarnate spirits from occultly possessed human beings and, indeed, on a much larger scale, planet Earth itself.

Many are those today who minimize or even nullify extremely valuable opportunities offered them by Servers. This they do by choosing to react in fear and ignorance to symptoms of their own potentially positive purification, instead of watching in wise detachment as psycho-emotional debris rises to the surface in order to be released. In thus blocking those impurities that need to be expelled, ignorant reactions serve only to inhibit what might otherwise be a most beneficial process of healing. Additionally, in giving energy to negative impulses by spitefully projecting the corresponding thoughts or emotions toward others, more unfavorable causes will be set up and shall have to be remedied at some future time. The Law of Karma is absolute, and each individual is wholly accountable for the reality which they create for themselves. Furthermore, and to one's greatest disadvantage, negative reactions may easily serve to attract the attention of unholy incorporeal beings, effectively opening the door to their adverse manipulations, and may ultimately lead to permanent possession by unseen preda-tors. A basic understanding of the occult laws operating behind the subtle energy dynamics experienced in human relationships is much needed today in these times of global cleansing. For now, a brief summary may serve to encourage the reader to investigate further.

Negative (or positive) thoughts and emotions (*thought-forms*) that are aimed at another person may only make a significant or long-term impression upon the intended recipient if in the aura of that individual there exists matter capable of responding sympa-thetically to the character of the directed energy. In the case where a thought-form is outside the range within which a person's con-sciousness is capable of resonating, the thought-form rebounds from it with a force proportional to the energy with which it was originally projected.* Hence the truism that a pure mind and heart are the best protection against inimical assaults of thought and feel-ing, for a pure mind and heart will maintain mental and emotional vehicles of fine and subtle matter, and such an aura will not respond to vibrations that require coarse and dense matter in order to find resonance. It is not difficult, then, to understand why all Servers would do well to recall these basic occult facts upon their Earthly mission today.

If an evil thought-form (i.e., one projected with malefic intent) strikes a purified body, it will rebound and fly back along the mag-netic line of least resistance, returning to and striking its creator. The originator, possessing mental and emotional matter in his aura that is sympathetic to that of the thought-form generated, is thrown into respondent vibrations, and suffers the destructive effects which he had intended to cause another. Thus, curses really do come home to roost, as the old saying goes. It may be clearly recog-nized, therefore, that to project hostile thoughts and feelings toward a Server (or, indeed, any well-meaning person for that mat-ter) is to invite immediate trouble for oneself in addition to the reg-ular, though perhaps more delayed, karmic repercussions of such

---

* It should be understood that a fraction of the potency of a neg-ative thought-form will always be experienced upon impact, even by the purest aura; Servers (especially those acting as energy transmuters) will certainly know that they are being attacked! However, as long as the recipient remains detached and free of conflicting ego reactions, then no lasting detrimen-tal effects will be sustained.

imprudent behavior. The reader is referred to the volume titles at the end of this book for further information regarding the hidden side of human relationships.

Awakened Servers are beginning to demonstrate today a universal principle: namely that when a member of the human race begins to approach the goal of Light and Wisdom (or 'Enlightenment' as it has been called by some older spiritual traditions), they automatically gain a field of influence that extends both up and down, which reaches both inwards toward the source of Light and outwards into the 'realms of darkness.' Once they have thus attained, they become a conscious centre of life-giving force, and are so without effort. Accomplished Servers will thus stimulate the advancement of all life with which they come into contact, and they will vivify that life by inducing in it a fresh evolutionary thrust, be it in human beings, other Servers, an animal, or even the living consciousness within the vegetable and mineral kingdoms. They will act as a transmitter of light in the darkness, naturally dispelling the illusions around them in order to let in the radiance of a brighter reality.

Awakened Servers, then, are practical occultists, and in transmitting positive energy they are able to bless those who are ready to receive it. The result of such beneficent transmissions will be dependent upon and directly proportional to a number of different factors. These are: i) the recipient's degree of openness and sincerity, ii) their genuine willingness to surrender all belief systems and attachments that no longer serve their greatest good, iii) their thirst to know a higher truth, iv) their degree of fearlessness and trust in life and, therefore, v) their readiness to learn and change, and to consequently move forward into greater spiritual awareness.

Energy transmissions may ensue without even a word being spoken to or by either the served or the Server, for it is the silent invocation of the receiving soul that spontaneously draws spiritual energy through the devoted personality of a Server, who in turn readily channels and radiates light from the higher planes. The personality of the recipient may comprehend little if anything of such a very positive dynamic, and, indeed, may find the whole affair rather bewildering, even affronting, seemingly having no prior knowledge of or conscious choice in the event. However, one's own inner consciousness, in being quite aware, certainly knows best, and it is this higher part of the recipient that decides whether it wishes to greet an aspect of the group-soul (the Server) on the physical plane.

The spiritualizing transmissions evoked by an awakened Server are designed to catalyze expanded states of consciousness in others so that they may be assisted in their own awakening and preparation for the forthcoming harvest. This phenomenon has the potential to instigate an important process of transmutation in the recipient, and might be regarded as a kind of *minor initiation* that may happen instantly upon meeting a Server or be realized at a later time when the seed planted at such an auspicious encounter begins to germinate amidst conducive mental and emotional conditions.

Such catalytic energy transmissions are an elementary demonstration of what might be regarded as *white magic*—a wielding of spiritual force for the benefit of others—in which most Servers have become thoroughly adept prior to their present incarnation. Today they are swiftly recalling these innate abilities, and, as might be expected, without the need for lengthy study or practise. However, Servers will ultimately recognize that they are only instruments of those metaphysical energies which they are able to conduct, as such transmissions are always effortless; they flow *through* the Server, not *from* them. The advantages received during such a vital interaction between two or more people are multiple, and all parties who have prepared themselves shall witness the wonderfully spiritualizing energies of divine providence surging through their consciousness as vibrations of love and healing descend from the higher worlds in gracious benediction. Such an experience exemplifies a universal law which ensures that when one serves another selflessly with concern only for the other person's greatest good, both parties are blessed, yet it is generally the servant who receives the most uplifting spiritual benefit.

Servers need to understand and remember always that if energy transmissions are to be maximally successful there must be a direct and unadulterated funneling of divine energy without significant distortion due to excitement, impassioned enthusiasm or inappropriate application by the person through which they are channelled. There often exist in the auras of awakening Servers certain unresolved personality imbalances that may inhibit or even corrupt the flow of pure spiritual energy which is available to them for helping others. However, such obstructions may be minimized and even completely dissolved when the Server remains calm, detached, humbly invocative, selfless and unconditionally loving.

As heralds, Servers represent the spiritual human being of the New World; they are the forerunners of the emerging new race upon Earth and are individually but tiny constituents of a great energy-distributing group. Acting as high-frequency energy transmitters, they are but tiny expressions of a vast process of transmutation that is currently underway within the galaxy, the solar system and upon Earth, and which is steadily expanding and intensifying. Servers thus offer, in advance, a stepped-down opportunity for purification and preparation to all those individuals who would ready themselves for the far greater inpouring of divine force, the advent of which is now so very close for our world. Such an early opportunity given by Servers has the potential to confer invaluable experience, insight and spiritual awakening. In light of that which now lies upon mankind's horizon, the benefits of such grace cannot be easily overstated.

6. As they awaken from their slumber (a process that will be discussed later in greater detail), the consciousness of the typical Server will evince itself as a natural, rapid and sympathetic response to suffering, power to comprehend principles easily, quick intuitions and keen perceptions. Thoroughness, a good sense of justice and dedication to Truth and righteousness will be amongst their recollected virtues, as will natural happiness, a contemplative intelligence, a pronounced passion to learn and an eagerness to help others. The innate intuitive and psychic abilities of Servers will reveal themselves through an increasing sensitivity to the influence of people and places, in the recalling of fragmentary memories of dream experiences and service while asleep, in greater responsiveness to direct guidance from the higher worlds, in the power to recognize the degree of spiritual attainment in others, in the ability to correctly interpret messages from Nature, and so forth.

7. A special and distinguishing mark of Servers is their recognition of the great need for unity, that prime ingredient that enables true spiritual fellowship to be realized, and which makes for discrimination, compassion and self-sacrifice. All that is narrow and exclusive, all that tends to separate one from another, that emphasizes differences instead of likenesses, is the antithesis of the Server on this, the eve of the birth of the New World. The essence of action by Servers is the union of many to achieve a single and selfless goal, not the dominance of one who is looked up to as a guru or saviour. Those Servers who shall lead humanity into the New World will do so in group formation and with empathy, insight and love, which will impel their philanthropic activity: *"By their fruits shall ye know them."* Metaphysical knowledge and compassion have ever guaran-

teed spiritual success, and working with, rather than against others is the mode of operation of all Servers who have remembered their duty. Those awakening servants of the race who have incarnated to exemplify the New World Consciousness today display a synthesizing spirit, being able to unite diversity of opinion and character, able to gather around them the most unlike elements and blend them into a collective, working whole for the greatest possible good.

The Veil of Forgetfulness

WITH THE RARE EXCEPTION of very advanced souls, the events of one's prenatal existence are governed by the Law of Forgetfulness. The physical plane is the only plane of forgetfulness, and this law is necessarily enforced for the vast majority of human incarnations in accordance with the unique learning opportunities available upon Earth. Third-density reality requires that those lives in physical embodiment should mature and grow subject to the law of free will, and the Law of Forgetfulness ensures that fresh choices are made in each new incarnation without recourse to the actual experiences of previous lifetimes. Prudent decisions independently made lead to more expeditious learning, and eventually to complete freedom from the need for further third-density experience. Such emancipation from the difficult but necessary and rewarding life-experience of the physical plane has in past been termed by some spiritual schools as 'Liberation,' and denotes a non-compulsory promotion from the dense material world and, therefore, a fortuitous movement forward in the eternal stream of spiritual unfoldment.

Now, all Servers who have chosen to incarnate physically upon Earth (even those who are here for the very first time) must adhere to the laws of the physical plane, and so during the earlier stages of their corporeal embodiment they are also subject to forgetfulness. This is another of the many burdens that Servers dutifully accept as an inherent factor in their voluntary descent into the vibratory fields of third-density existence. The veil of forgetfulness is designed to mask the memory of their origins, purpose on Earth, higher consciousness, etc., to the degree necessary for them to experience fully the typical human condition. It also affords them needed camouflage until it is time for their public recognition. However, the veil does not inhibit all of their sensibilities, and this is why most Servers will feel alienated within society to some degree, for they sense that there is so much more to life than that of which humanity is aware, and they often suffer painful lessons in order to arrive at the definite acknowledgement that Truth and divine Love are generally quite unknown and unpopular strangers here upon Earth.

The personal veil imposes certain restrictions upon the soul that frequently serve to evoke a common pattern throughout the lives of Servers. This pattern often includes trials and challenges that may produce considerable friction and distress for Servers up until their circumstances become better understood by penetrating the veil to some degree. Generally, difficulties will repeat themselves until Servers have learned necessary lessons by way of their physical incarnation and so become qualified to empathically assist humanity. One of the most significant distinctions of the dense material world in comparison to the more subtle spheres is that it offers repeated opportunities to learn how to love unconditionally despite its abundant dualities and illusions, and Servers are generally inhibited from remembering who they are until they choose to use their free will wisely by loving and helping others. This last point is of vital importance and is most worthy of serious consideration by anyone who is beginning to suspect their nature and, therefore, their purpose upon Earth.

As necessary as the veil of forgetfulness is to the overall success of each Server's mission, the masked condition is designed to be but temporary. Servers invariably possess certain inner senses which, when heeded, will always impel them to serve the directives of the group-soul rather than those of the personality, and in order to penetrate the veil of forgetfulness and so consciously remember their duty, Servers must *listen* carefully within; they must *trust* their Greater Self, and then *act* upon their insights and true spiritual impulses. It is the duty of all Servers to ultimately negate the mandatory imposition made upon them by the veil, and they may hasten this important process of awakening by applying in their lives two rudimentary measures: i) sincere and intelligent seeking of Truth, and ii) active service. By law, both these activities, if done in earnest, will ensure assistance from the invisible worlds, and so help lead Servers into a progressive emergence from the veiled condition.

It should be remembered that Servers have already reached a higher level of spiritual attainment than the average Earth-bound soul. Therefore, the physical, emotional and mental components of the individual that together comprise the personality of the Server are to be regarded solely as the *lower vehicles* of expression, communication and service. However, in accord with the Law of Forgetfulness, once new vehicles are taken on in physical incarnation the veil must be pierced anew, self-knowledge reattained and divine contact re-established as a personality before real spiritual service may be rendered. Therefore, the art of spiritual discrimination must be recultivated by incarnated Servers in order to help effect purification of the lower vehicles which, without exception, will have become tainted by the polluted ethers and countless other detrimental influences upon Earth. Purification is a process that must be furthered every day in order that the veil of forgetfulness may be progressively attenuated as higher spiritual contact is fostered. Negative purification, i.e., the release of harmful patterns from the emotional body, and positive purification, i.e., the education of the mental body, will bring about the balanced preparation of the Server's personality, rapport with the group-soul and so also with the Divine Plan. This process of alignment and purification is essential both to the thinning of the veil and the fortification of the Server's vehicles so that they may be prepared for contact with Divinity, and the way of purification exemplified by Servers is a road upon which humanity must also embark if it is to enter the New World. In helping to liberate humanity from the prison of self, such alignment of the personality with the purposes of the divine Will is the goal of all Servers today, and shall enable the Law of Service to be progressively and spontaneously demonstrated upon Earth.

* * *

There exist certain personal benefits to the veil of forgetfulness also. Firstly, it restricts the amount of inflowing force or *home-vibration* until the personality is ready to receive it, able to take responsibility for the consequences of such power, and thus to wield it safely in the world for the good of others. Secondly, the potent effects created prematurely by a high-frequency aura upon Earth would undoubtedly result in excessive persecution from those who do not possess spiritual understanding. An unveiled personality in the public arena would thus suffer inordinately at the hands of many human beings who would become quite dazzled by an awakened Server's innate radiance. Mankind is still not ready today to behold the full light of the New World Consciousness, the precipitation of which shall be introduced to Earth via the lower vehicles of Servers. Therefore, the veil is left intact to some degree until the right moment, and this also provides opportunity for further preparation by the personalities of Servers, as sufficient strength, confidence and wisdom is regained from their experience in physical incarnation.

However, the more diligent and advanced among Servers are today successfully penetrating their veil of forgetfulness to a significant degree, and are consequently attaining at least a fragmentary recollection of their mission. However, should these awakened ones choose to ignore their newly-recalled spiritual duty to humanity, and instead fall prey, even to a small extent, to selfishness under the surreptitious influence of those materialistic forces that still hold sway over the Earth, they will subsequently suffer hefty penalties that will be imposed upon their personality by their own group-soul in order to encourage them back along the right road. Such consequences are often quite disturbing for Servers who may find that they have plunged to an all-time low of depression, confusion or worse, whereby no light may be found by them anywhere. Such a quandary will last for as long as they continue to live for self and not for others. These measures may appear to be somewhat severe when regarded casually, yet they are actually a part of the Servers' *basic training*, implemented by no other factor save the directives of their group-soul in order that their future service may be carried out according to plan. Such measures may be rightfully recognized, therefore, as being most appropriate when considering the important task of Servers which, in being a part of the Divine Plan for mankind on Earth at this critical time, must be given every opportunity to succeed. Servers who may have become lost in a cloud of personal problems may profit by contemplating their attitudes and reactions to all phenomena related to their malaise until they uncover what life has been whispering to them by way of their disquietude.

The planetary deadline is so very close today that recent arrivals among Servers necessarily carry a thinner veil of forgetfulness, and will consequently witness far less limitation imposed upon them. The awakening and positive engagement of these more youthful Servers will also be better facilitated than their predecessors because their innate spiritual faculties and teaching skills will be better recognized, appreciated, more enthusiastically evoked and consciously required by a more awakened and readied humanity whose attentiveness to the laws of life will have been galvanized by crisis during the rapidly changing and climactic times ahead.

The Imitation Ego

AGES AGO, when it was first decided to send divine emissaries to this world, Server group-souls looked down upon planet Earth and selected their grand mission-objective. They observed areas of potential and need, and, based upon their own aptitudes and proclivities, they chose to despatch fragments of themselves into third-density reality. These early Servers did not possess any physical-plane karma, for they had previously learned and transcended the lessons of third-density consciousness long ago. Thus they were not required by law to take a physical body at all. However, in order to render a complete service upon Earth, a corporeal embodiment was necessary for some among their number. Therefore, the original incarnating Servers assumed temporary personalities which, unlike those belonging to the great majority of Earth-bound souls, did not contain many seeds of personal karma* accrued upon the lower planes, and today, as far as the group-soul is concerned, a Server's lower vehicles of consciousness are still strictly utilitarian, and so for the sake of conceptual convenience might be termed a *false* or *imitation* ego.

Of course, all egos are essentially 'false' in the sense that they are temporary vehicles of the soul utilized for its karmic resolution. All human egos begin to dissolve upon physical death as the various elements that constitute the personality—physical, etheric, emotional and mental—gradually disintegrate and are returned to the general pool of matter on their corresponding planes, while the divine spark gradually withdraws itself from the grosser densities on its return journey inwards. Due to the nature of its essential purpose, however, the Server's ego may be regarded as false or imitation when compared to that of the ordinary reincarnating life on Earth, which is still attached to the *wheel of rebirth,* and also due to the fact that once that purpose is accomplished successfully—either in one or, more usually, over numerous incarnations—the Server's lower vehicles will dis-

---

* Whenever an aspect of an advanced group-soul chooses to incarnate in third density by way of the normal process of physical birth, certain constraints and karmic taints are necessarily adopted under the Law of Reincarnation. However, such impediments may be rapidly transmuted by the higher vibratory frequency of the indwelling consciousness.

solve permanently, never to be reconstituted. If, however, the Server later volunteers for another physical-plane assignment, a brand new personality would be created as a vehicle of expression in the lower worlds, to be eventually discarded yet again once its function was complete; and so it is that age after age, cycle after cycle, the group-soul takes up and casts off its physical, emotional and mental garments through which it incarnates in order to meet the ever-changing demands of the Universal Divine Plan in many different worlds.

An integral part of the Servers' mission upon Earth throughout history and to date has been to utilize the imitation ego in order to make experiential contact with the complete spectrum of worldly disharmony, and to suffer all levels of human affliction and pain so that every discordant energy upon the planet might become absorbed by their lower vehicles, therefore connecting them to the Earth's collective consciousness. It is thus that Servers gain the ability to assist in the transmutation of human karma on a planetary scale. Accordingly, over time, the Servers have incarnated into every part of the world, and, between them, have taken on every kind of burden and malady known to mankind. They have become intimately acquainted with all the various forms of suffering upon Earth, as during the course of numerous terrestrial lifetimes they have been born into every conceivable dysfunctional situation on the planet; into lives of abuse, neglect, poverty, disease, corruption, war and so on, and herein lies one of their greatest challenges, for in egoic-identification upon Earth lie many difficulties and pitfalls.

The instant an individual thinks of the separated personality (one's own or that of others), false or at best limited identification is made, and that person's choice automatically segregates him from the greater, truer life of spiritual inclusivity. Whenever one's consciousness is conditioned by the lower self—its feelings, reactions, desires, failures, successes, etc.—one becomes subject to spiritual blindness and the subsequent suffering that must ensue as a result, for such is the lot of the separate self. The Server's preoccupation with the imitation ego is the single most powerful impediment to establishing divine contact, and is essentially, therefore, a major source of their pain and conflict. Identification with the imitation ego will always create distortions of those true soul-memories which may be recalled by the Server, and this may lead them to believe that they need to search for solutions to their own inner conflicts in the outside world amongst the plethora of so-called spiritual paths and techniques of mystical enlighten-ment that abound today. This misconception can lead to much frustration and disappointment for the Server due to the fact that precious few established spiritual or religious 'authorities' under-stand precisely what is presently transpiring upon Earth with regard to the unique circumstances pertaining to Servers, and therefore are unable to offer appropriate counsel with regard to the special condition and requirements of the imitation ego. Con-sequently, unaware Servers may often find themselves quite bewildered and lost amidst the escalating distortions and self-seeking glamors that are everywhere apparent within the spiri-tual supermarket today. Neither the great majority of hyped New Age information nor religious tradition holds the key to the pecu-liar circumstances facing Servers in the world at this particular time.

It would be most advantageous indeed for Servers to attain a basic comprehension of the occult constitution of man, as such self-knowledge will help them in understanding and thus intelli-gently directing their lower vehicles of consciousness instead of becoming blindly controlled by them in their forgetfulness, as humanity generally allows itself to be. Physical instruments are required by the various spiritual Hierarchies (who are predomi-nantly resident upon the inner planes) in order to channel high-frequency transmutative energies into the material world. The imitation ego, when rightly utilized, forms a centre for the trans-formation (stepping down) and transmission of such divine forces. Integrated personalities provide a bridge between the higher and the lower worlds, between humanity and the Hierar-chies. However, excessive association with the imitation ego as being the real self bears significant danger, for the consequent contraction of consciousness will inevitably lead to doubt, fear, struggle and unloving thought and action, and will subsequently create new and undesirable karma, thereby effectively rendering the imitation ego 'real.' By law, such newly acquired karma must be cleared before Servers are able to: i) restore full remembrance upon Earth of their spiritual status and duty, ii) effect their mis-sion successfully, and iii) return home (or proceed beyond) after having completed the purpose of their incarnation(s).

Servers in embodiment upon Earth today are certainly not the first to experience such spiritual trials, for many great pioneers have gone before them, traversed the *vale of tears* and in the end have triumphed. For example, Jesus repeatedly wrestled with his own veil of forgetfulness, and, like present-day Servers, possessed an imitation ego. He also had to learn to discriminate between the two distinct parts of his being of which he became conscious: the divine and the human. Due to his uncompromising identification with the world of Spirit—*"my Father's Kingdom"*—and as a result of his unselfish dedication to humanity's salvation, he underwent the transformational process of initiation that ultimately led him to complete remembrance upon Mount Calvary on the cross where he uttered his final words of victory, *"Eloi, Eloi, lamah shavahhtani: Elohim, Elohim, how dost Thou glorify me,"* and *"Consummatum Est: It is finished."* The process of initiation—symbolized in Jesus' life as the birth, baptism, transfiguration, crucifixion, resurrection and ascension—is more ancient than humanity itself, and by his perfect demonstration of the Way, Jesus made known publicly the one True Path that leads from darkness to Light. It is this same road down which all successful Servers and humanity must pass today in order to enter *The Kingdom of Heaven;* yet not alone as did Jesus, but collectively, for the Passion Play of the Aquarian age—The Return of Christ—is one of a far greater magnitude than Jesus' solitary example. As the Piscean Christ himself averred nearly 2,000 years ago, *"Greater works than these shall ye do."*—John 14:12 (paraphrased).

* * *

There is a little-known yet vitally important condition that is unique to the imitation ego and which, once fully understood and so rightly identified, will relieve Servers of much confusion, doubt and worry.

Our Milky-Way galaxy with its myriad planes and sub-planes is a vast sphere of life comprising countless developing lives and civilizations. A huge number of these lives are most aware of the momentous nature of what is unfolding upon Earth today, and they are either karmically or otherwise magnetized to partake to some degree in the experience of our planet's transition. Yet if just one single representative from every interested civilization in the galaxy were to incarnate in our physical world, there would not be enough standing space for them!

These emissaries, then, could not all incarnate on Earth as individual human beings (starseeds), for there is simply not enough room on the planet. Therefore, a great number of them are today 'hitching a ride,' as it were, within the consciousness of strategically-incarnating Servers, and this was voluntarily agreed to by the Servers themselves upon their descent into this world.

Within the personality vehicles of an individual Server, therefore, one may witness many 'different colored threads'* that connect to numerous and diverse galactic civilizations and races from various worlds and densities, all of whom have access, via the imitation ego, to all that Gaia is and will be experiencing during this time of planetary transformation. Therefore, the advanced Server on Earth at this time will be carrying a variety of *holographic points of consciousness* on behalf of certain civilizations as a kind of 'composite envoy' on Earth, a *surrogate* for them.

These living, vibrating, experiencing threads of consciousness double as 'access portals' to many other worlds for the Server's personal consciousness itself. Being unintegrated, unenlightened, not yet liberated from matter, the civilizations that Servers carry are right here on Earth today in time and space courtesy of the Servers' voluntary mission, and are, through them, seeking learning, healing, spiritual stimulation and ultimately Liberation. As well as experiencing this planet's density together with all its unique lessons, these civilizations are also ever seeking to communicate through Servers *to* this world and to the various threads of consciousness that are operating in and through other physically-incarnated Servers and starseeds here on Earth at this time. (It is not such an uncommon experience that certain individuals report seeing 'other worlds' in some people's eyes!).

As Servers awaken, then, and so regain access to higher levels of their being they will become a very busy nexus of galactic activity, a microcosmic expression of both the galaxy as well as Mother Earth herself at this time, for the planet is presently acting as a kind of interdimensional, interstellar communication station and integration portal connecting a great plexus of life-waves all throughout the ring-pass-not of this galaxy.

The threads within the Servers' imitation egos tie their souls to various levels of consciousness belonging to spiritual beings whose journey towards Liberation from matter is not yet complete, and at some stage it will be clearly observed that neither are some of them very happy! Their home-frequency is not in harmony with the divine Kingdom to which they are seeking to return with the help

---

* Such threads are adopted *in addition* to the normal karmic threads that each incarnating life necessarily inherits via the blood of their parents.

of Servers on Earth. Such threads of consciousness can often be quite noisy, restless, quarrelsome (amongst themselves and with the Server) and so definitely unintegrated and in need of love, wisdom and guidance. They are, therefore, not yet free of fear and ignorance, and they will be vying for the Servers' attention more and more as the planetary tempo quickens. Hence, during the intensifying maelstrom of these "last days" it is very important for Servers to maintain a True and Holy Focus; to simplify their lives as they *"make straight the paths of the Lord"* within their imitation egos by remembering a purely vertical, selflessly dedicated and unconditional aspiration to serve the Divine Plan on behalf of both their civilizations *and* humanity. The degree to which a Server progresses in purity towards holy transfiguration during the forthcoming influx of the Grace of an Age, will directly and proportionately assist the *lambs of God* within them, guiding them toward the Fold.

Servers will generally continue to experience the karma and struggles of their civilization-threads right up until Judgement Day. The Servers have many 'children' who are looking to them for help and direction, and a part of their personal mission is to encourage these 'dependents' to come Home with them through the Christine Gate. However, with so many inner (psychic) and outer (worldly) threads pushing and tugging at the Servers' lower consciousness during the impending Earthly storms, things may become quite confusing for them at times, yet only if Servers allow themselves, by wrong identification, to get caught up in the cyclone that is a necessary corollary of the planetary cleansing. A True Focus will allow Servers to remain in the centre of the cyclone of agitated dualistic conditions in these times, remaining balanced, tranquil, unmovable and untouchable by the greatest waves of fear and doubt that are rising up in the world today.

* * *

Upon the right identification of their personality as but an instrument of service depends the success of each individual Server's mission. Indeed, a distinguishing mark of awakened Servers with karmically uncontaminated imitation egos is an attitude toward their personal life as representing just a tiny aspect of a far greater collective function and experience. In this way their relationship to life remains distinctly impersonal, and so they are able to view the world through spiritual eyes. Ken Carey sums up the essential need for such an attitude in the following words (spoken by Christ): *"Whoever will come after Me will have to die to all definitions of self . . . Whoever clings to his definition of self will lose his identity when that definition is no more, but whoever shall relinquish all definitions for My sake, and for the entry of My consciousness, the same will share in My eternal life."* —The Starseed Transmissions.

Personal identification with any threads or complexes of the imitation ego obstructs intuition and will inevitably lead to confusion, misguided effort and, therefore, inappropriate action, which shall do more damage than good to the Server, their mission and to those whom they may attempt to help. Many Servers today are grasping at certain bold and unnecessarily complex ideals as they rush forward into a service which their distorted yet essentially true senses inform them that they ought to be doing. Amidst the confusion of their hasty altruism and impatience they may contribute toward much disorder in a world that is already inundated by a torrent of misinformation scattered abroad by the excited and zealous. The way of the Spirit has always been most simple, clear and straightforward, yet today many Servers are unwittingly following humanity's wayward example by incorporating into their lives all kinds of elaborate schemes, rituals and practises, ostensibly in order to 'meet the demands of the New Age' and to be assured of a place amongst those who will know success during the times ahead. A deluge of very intriguing notions, plans and new techniques with which to attain self-liberation, empowerment and personal ascension proliferate in the world today, and these tend to distract the mass of humanity from the simple Truth, therefore leading many away from the True Path and contaminating even the minds of awakening Servers with various falsehoods.

Erroneous thinking may be swiftly rectified, however, by the acquisition of Right Knowledge, which shall subsequently reveal that only in the crucible of selfless service can the illusions built up by the imitation ego be transmuted, as the corresponding invocational influx of divine Light purifies and uplifts all life that it touches. In attuning correctly to the new and higher frequencies of energy now available on Earth, and in learning from and relinquishing all past misconceptions and false identifications, the Server's consciousness will indubitably expand as all past experiences become illumined by the lamp of Insight. Such clarity of perception will then promote a new awareness of the lessons contained but overlooked in past error (nothing is ever wasted), and it simultaneously avails Servers a recognition of their usefulness in future service as their vision grows. It may be seen, then, that each moment presents anew the opportunity to either purify (prepare) or taint (hinder) the imitation ego depending upon the Server's identification, focus and motivations.

While the Servers' veiled condition allows them to gain a first-hand experience—via the imitation ego—of all the separation and despair in the world, at the same time and at a level of knowing beyond the veil of forgetfulness and at the heart of the group-soul, they have ever been aware that their suffering was for others and but temporary. Many Servers retain a vestige of memory from early infancy that a time will come—and soon—when everything will change *"in the twinkling of an eye,"* and that the imitation ego will become completely transparent in the final stage of their mission; the temporary personality shed and discarded like the cocoon of a butterfly having served its purpose.

Eventually, on the *Day of Remembrance*, Servers will again realize upon this, their current, and for many, concluding assignment upon Earth, that their true Self is far more than their imitation ego. Meanwhile, as they evolve from their preoccupation with the personality, the Servers' reality will grow progressively broader, for in their expanding perceptions they will be able to behold more and more of the divine grandeur, beauty, interconnectivity and magnificent all-pervading intelligence of Creation. Following the piercing of the veil of forgetfulness—attained only through purification of the imitation ego in world service—the personal self will dissolve, merge and become fully united once again with the group-soul, while lifting every painful Earthly experience into the light of transmutation. By way of the Law of Synthesis, humanity's long-standing condition of suffering will thus be remedied as the entire planet is positively transformed. Surely there can be no greater honour and joy in the whole world such as this. Indeed, at this momentous time of completion, so intense will be the exhilaration of Servers, so profound their bliss, and so ineffably spiritual the experience of divine reward, that each and every soul without exception would gladly repeat the same sacrifice in service all over again. Such a consecrated attitude is mentioned in John's Book of Revelation in the New Testament when: *"… the four and twenty elders throw their crowns* [halos] *down in front of the throne of God."*—Rev. 4:10.

The Waiting Period

THE EARTH-TRANSFORMATION of greatest consequence will take place most swiftly and will be a tangibly objective result of that which has already transpired within the higher worlds. The stepping-up of the planetary frequency has, up to this time, been gradual and relatively subtle; its effects have even passed unnoticed to date by many people. However, it is the *rending of the veil between worlds* that is sudden, and not the developments of the preparatory stages leading up to the great shift.

The duration of the period up until the planetary deadline and the prophesied shift in global consciousness is dependent upon a multitude of variables ranging from interstellar and interdimensional activity right down to the thoughts and actions of humanity; everything and everyone is connected and interdependent. Many Servers are today waiting in conscious anticipation for others to find their positions and to ready themselves in order to welcome together to Earth that great Light which is already poised upon the horizon of the old world. Some physically-incarnated Servers have waited patiently (and others, frustratingly!) for decades as the greater unfoldment of the Divine Plan for Earth has been repeatedly delayed due to the pervasive planetary domination by materialistic forces, and, therefore, humanity's lack of preparedness.

The more awakened Servers may sometimes retain certain impressions from their dynamically service-oriented multidimensional life, which are often recalled from dreams, and since they sense in their relatively limited waking state that they actually possess a much broader awareness, spiritual activity and sphere of positive influence than they are able to demonstrate in their everyday terrestrial existence, they often harbour a deep longing to proceed at full speed upon the physical plane also. Yet, as previously mentioned, the world is still not ready, and during the waiting period Servers may consequently and quite understandably feel somewhat ineffective or even redundant in their physical bodies while in ordinary third-density consciousness. However, regardless of how desperately they may try, no matter what spiritual disciplines they may diligently practise, and despite how many rituals or prayers they may perform, Servers are unable to bring their highest faculties and greater spiritual awareness down into physical objectivity before the appointed time when all will stand in readiness, and, for most, their mission unfolds on a strictly need-to-know basis. In part, the gross vibrations that are still prevalent upon Earth today prevent the Servers' greater consciousness from manifesting, yet once the group-soul is girded and ready, when the required number of world Servers are in their place, when the planetary deadline has been reached, and when the waiting period finally comes to an end, a torrential inpouring of divine force will catalyze the dawning of a supreme Power and Intelligence in those who have prepared themselves adequately to receive and transmit such Light. Meanwhile, the unawakened Servers' life pattern generally reflects on many levels the typical condition of humanity before its own destined awakening.

The waiting period may be regarded as the preliminary stage of the Servers' intelligently-unfolding mission, whereby preparation is made—mainly upon the inner side of life—for a full spiritual awakening, via the personality upon the physical plane, where a significant increase in activity and service will subsequently result. Frequently, this period of waiting for Servers is tainted by anxiety, frustration, bewilderment, doubt, alienation, lack of direction and purpose, and, of course, all the other usual concerns and woes that similarly plague humanity. Such afflictions are often particularly poignant for Servers, however, due to reasons already discussed. The gross psychic atmosphere upon Earth that holds down the field of human consciousness within which they have volunteered to incarnate will feel like a veritable prison to most awakening Servers. They may also discover that they become at least tacitly outcast from and by society, for as their awareness unfolds and their remembrance is restored they will find it impossible to fit into social systems that are set against the principles of harmony, spiritual progress and divine purpose.

Greater numbers of Servers today are realizing just how markedly incompatible are their own ethics and spiritual ideals when compared to the commonly-accepted and established world standards. Standing with the spiritual Sun behind them, the shadows of the world become accentuated in the Servers' perception; they are able to see what others cannot. In therefore being acutely aware of humanity's suffering on all levels, and in beholding negativity and escalating imbalance everywhere in the world, Servers may become coerced by their divine sense of Right to reject the present systems of government and livelihood altogether, even while lacking suitable alternative means of survival. Due to their innate clarity of perception, their sensitivity, integrity and well-meaning propensity to reveal the Truth while living in a land of lies, Servers are often subject to all kinds of struggles and persecution during the waiting period; difficulties which, nonetheless, are guaranteed to yield most favorable results when faced and overcome. In meeting the challenges of the waiting period with faith, understanding, fortitude and patience, the ability to express love unreservedly toward all the multifarious manifestations of the physical world will become natural and spontaneous.

Challenges for Servers in the waiting period, then, are certainly not wanting. However, in terms of spiritual opportunity these challenges are most useful. In fact, they are sometimes specifically designed and presented by the intelligence of the group-soul in order to evoke the employment of free will in choosing to begin the important process of seeking solutions and to subsequently make further choices based upon the knowledge and experience gained from that search, just as humanity has to do if it is to change its present pitiable condition. In receiving the knocks and bruises from the experiences of life upon Earth during the waiting period, it is anticipated by the group-soul that Servers will proceed toward a deeper understanding of the nature of mankind's problems and, therefore, obtain a firm grasp of the demands to be met for the successful execution of their collective mission of world service. Although the waiting period may seem cumbersome and slow to many, Servers would do well not to underestimate the importance of this time in which they may lay the foundations of their greater future duty to humanity. *"He who is faithful in that which is least is faithful also in much. No initiate has ever passed the great test of initiation who has not accustomed himself to pass lesser tests every day of his life."*—The Tibetan Master, Djwhal Khul.

Due to their temporary yet very real human limitations, Servers are ever tempted to repeat the same habitual mistakes made by mankind. The path of least resistance is a well-trodden and easy road, and some Servers will find that they have also strayed onto the path of thorns that leads into a darkened land fraught with both dangers and hard but necessary lessons. However, those Servers who shall know victory upon their mission will eventually cease to tread what is known in esoteric circles as the *left-hand path*: the way of service to self. They must, at some time during the waiting period, come to realize that as long as they choose to imitate humanity in identifying and struggling with the problems of the lower self, or personality, they will never find a way out of their loneliness and suffering, for they are looking in the wrong direction! Successful Servers will discover that their personal anguish and world-weariness will dissolve once they recall how to triumph over the burden that all humanity bears; a burden which has accumulated over ages of perpetual selfishness and ignorance. Servers must remember that liberation from personal suffering is attained only when identification with the greater suffering of the human family (and of all life upon Earth) is made, and thus true Compassion is awakened. The mighty spiritual power and infallible wisdom of the group-soul is made available to the Server who is able to rise above the ordinary world of the personality in thought as well as deed, and so live for a greater cause than merely their own happiness. *"If you would give your life for the selfish self, then you will lose your life. If you will give your life in service to your fellow men, then you will save your life. If you would find the spirit life, the life of man in God, then you must walk a narrow way and enter through a narrow gate."*—Jesus.

Third-density experience in the waiting period presents multiple occasions to learn how to love through the seemingly impenetrable illusion of separation. It does this by imparting its lessons by way of the particular obstacles and hardships that only the physical plane can provide. However difficult such lessons may be, they do offer a commensurate spectrum of opportunities for expeditious growth and, therefore, conscious spiritual advancement. Education on the physical plane ultimately bestows upon successful souls their rightfully-earned passage into higher, more expansive levels of experience. Thus, for an Earth-bound soul who has for the first time balanced all third-density karma and learned adequately the lessons of the physical plane, their development will continue in more subtle realms with full continuity of consciousness from one incorporeal incarnation to the next. For the successful Server on assignment upon planet Earth, rewards are, of course, greater, and apply differently due to the higher turn of the evolutionary spiral that they have already reached prior to their Earthly mission.

* * *

It is to be observed today during the waiting period that a significant number of awakening Servers are assuming an unjustified satisfaction in their partially-remembered spiritual status, and this is a cause for concern. Those who become aware of vague soul-memories sometimes misinterpret them and become convinced that they need not subscribe wholly to the laws and realities that pertain to the physical plane. Such misapprehension of states of consciousness that are real and valid only in the absence of the lower, personality vehicles is today responsible for much imprudent complacency amongst Servers. Therefore, delay in the execution of their mission is known as complications arise and new karma is created. Instead of wilfully and intelligently penetrating the veil of forgetfulness by seeking and serving, Servers sometimes take too much comfort and security in their sense that 'something wonderful is approaching' and that they need do nothing but 'wait for the party to begin!' While such prescience does indeed contain an underlying truth, smugness together with its corresponding spiritual passivity will not conduce toward the Servers' adequate preparation, and so will certainly detract from the purpose of their incarnation. Self-satisfaction amongst Servers in the waiting period is, of course, most unhelpful to the furtherance of raising the planetary vibration, and may also ultimately leave their vehicles unfit to receive the powerful spiritual energies that are soon to be released in the world.

The personalities that the group-soul inhabits constitute vital instruments through which the directives of the Divine Plan may manifest upon Earth. Therefore, Servers will wish to keep their mental, emotional and physical bodies in the best possible condition in order that an optimum service may be accomplished through them; a service that the Servers' greater multidimensional consciousness perpetually renders upon many planes simultaneously on the other side of the veil between worlds. Servers who choose to ignore the lessons offered them within the waiting period (like those of humanity who today opt to remain selfish and spiritually inert) are much more likely to witness the negative effects of the incoming streams of Aquarian energy, the nature of which is purificatory. Servers should bear in mind that since they are generally more sensitive than the average person, they will experience the effects of the inflowing energies first, and also that if they do not prepare adequately in the time preceding the planetary deadline, then they may fail humanity as well as their own group-soul to the same degree as that of their own neglect. Furthermore, and due to their inherent understanding, Servers are duty-bound to offer their knowledge to humanity. If complacency or indifference forestalls them from effecting that duty, then they contravene the Law of Service by which their souls live. In thus denying their own spirit, they inevitably suffer and may incur further karmic penalties.

The waiting period is an important time for Servers to learn to transcend their doubts and fears, and to subsequently begin acting interdependently with one another and humanity for a worthy cause. During the waiting period the typical Server's temporary limitations, imposed by the veil of forgetfulness, compel them to unite and to form cooperative groups whereby their diverse but complementary skills may be employed to help manifest the group-vision. In offering themselves up once again as surrendered instruments of the divine Will, the process of their own spiritual reawakening—their remembrance—will automatically unfold.

There are other advantages to be realized within the waiting period also. Although these may sometimes be regarded as lesser forms of service, they are of important consequence within the overall mission of the individual Server and should not be overlooked. They include:

1. **Preparation of the way** for others by exemplifying the essential requirement on the spiritual path of a humbly-seeking attitude. Earnest enquiry into the truth of the times and the purpose of their incarnation will inevitably avail Servers of necessary insight and experience, and this will, in turn, lead to the attainment of conviction born of an adequate comprehension of those subtle senses that were previously but vague whispers from the soul within. In thus acquiring a truer understanding of their place within the Divine Plan for planet Earth and in gaining an appreciation of their potential contribution toward the furtherance of that Plan, the spirit of the Server will begin to confidently manifest itself once more in waking consciousness, synthesizing and integrating into one cohesive whole the knowledge and experience of past lifetimes together with that of the present incarnation.

2. **The registering for posterity of important discoveries** and realizations upon the path of seeking in all areas of human innovation, and the collation of those observations and events for the absorption of the group mind, thereafter becoming a part of its cumulative experience and understanding.

3. **Raising the planetary vibration.** By their very presence, and even while still in the veiled condition, the auric fields of Servers—having a higher-than-normal vibratory rate—will assist in the transmutation of gross energies around the world. Additionally, in striving for spiritual understanding, the Server will further contribute toward the good of the whole by radiating helpful and stimulating energies along their path.

4. **Inspiring humanity to fresh efforts** in its own search for Truth, while simultaneously helping to recall to their purpose other tarrying Servers whose veil of forgetfulness may not yet have been penetrated in any significant way.

5. **The transmutation and activation of the Earth's subtle energy grid.** Servers often find themselves responding to an inner compulsion to visit various places in the world. Sometimes these locations reveal themselves to be established, forgotten or undiscovered sacred sites where the Server may spontaneously—consciously or unconsciously—assist in preparing Mother Earth for her imminent rebirth by helping to release important data and vital energies that are stored within the planetary intelligence, and which are essentially related to the impending great shift.

6. **Living the new world paradigm and, therefore, demonstrating the practicality of manifesting the true vision of the Aquarian age.** As everything belonging to the old and outmoded world standards atrophies, approaching eventual collapse and complete disintegration, Servers will lead the way into the New World by willingly sacrificing those material securities and typical social comforts that have become the norm for so many today in the West. In exchange they will actively embrace a greater Cause: the furtherance of the One Divine Work upon Earth.

7. **Galvanizing others to move forward on the spiritual path** by offering a field of service to all.

8. **Generally assisting in the re-education of humanity** in preparation for the New Day.

The majority of these services during the earlier stages of a Server's mission and before the all-important Harvest Time are preliminary and so will not be rendered indefinitely. Indeed, they may generally only be effected in the waiting period and before full remembrance for the following reasons:

i.   As the veil of forgetfulness is attenuated and awakening ensues, the auric fields of Servers will become highly magnetized. Consequently, the regular contact and relationship that may have previously been practicable with the mass of humanity will become progressively inexpedient due to incompatibility of vibration. The more intense and powerful emanations of the Server in the near future will cause problems for those who remain in hiding within the shadows of selfishness and fear.

ii. As they recall their collective purpose and consequently undergo the restoration of their innate higher faculties, Servers will necessarily become more dedicated and specialized in their field of service, and are much more likely to withdraw from the world at large for more vital esoteric work in closed circles.

iii. As vibratory frequencies are increasing today upon Earth, darkness is becoming magnified in the world as antagonistic forces make their final and desperate attempt to maintain control and domination. As all humanity continues to be coerced to face and deal with its inner impurity, the inherent and growing hypersensitivity of Servers will coerce their retreat from the intensifying maelstrom of global catharsis. The more remembrance that Servers attain, the more will they be distanced from those of humanity who fail to choose love and service as a way of life. In fact, in the very near future, one way or another, each individual upon Earth will have made a necessary choice to affiliate with either the *Islands of Light* or the *caverns of darkness*; there will be no grey areas.

* * *

The patience of Servers is very often pushed to the limit in the waiting period, for in their homesickness many feel quite ready to return to their native world. However, Servers certainly did not incarnate upon Earth merely to turn around and return home before first successfully effecting their mission. Servers who make expedient choices during the waiting period should be encouraged by the fact that the latter phase of their mission will prove to be so much more tangibly positive, joyful and productive than the initial stage of inevitable blindness and struggle. The greater details of their noble duty to mankind and planet Earth will very soon be recalled by successful Servers, as their mission is accomplished in complete remembrance.

Meanwhile, *do not identify with this transient dream-life*. These are ever the watchwords of the Server during the waiting period, for as objectivity is maintained in all things—keeping eyes, ears, mind and heart open—it will be observed that everything in the world is in a tangible state of flux, with much greater change still to come. The concerns and anxieties of yesterday's reality may be regarded retrospectively as just a fleeting chimera in the light of a new and brighter reality today. Servers who have to date persevered in their duty with grim determination, and who may have grown weary, feeling as if they might expire from sheer loneliness and isolation in a foreign and hostile land, need struggle alone no longer, for the good news is now abroad, and an ever increasing number of Servers are awakening today, and are seeking to reunite.

Progressive contact with the group-soul is presently being attained by those Servers who have learned the lessons of their waiting period, and who are, therefore, able to understand, accept, forgive and release their past, thereby dissolving any accumulated bonds of third-density karma. Thus freed, they may begin to arise effortlessly upon the ever-new inflowing waves of spiritual opportunity. As more Servers are awakening and embarking consciously upon the path of seeking and service today, they are attracting to themselves other individuals who belong to their own immediate spiritual family as well as questing members of humanity. On a global scale, the speed with which the inevitable process of regrouping upon the physical plane progresses determines the time of the accomplishment of the great collective function that Servers have incarnated to execute in the world and, therefore, also affect the duration of the waiting period.

Wake-up Calls

ALL SERVERS possess what may be regarded metaphorically as a kind of inner time-clock that has been set to arouse their consciousness from its mission-imposed slumber at the appointed hour when they will be required to act in the world with greater spiritual effect. Received as either internal impulses triggered from hidden dimensions or as catalysts originating from the external world, wake-up calls will sound at different times for each individual Server as they tread their path, and later for larger numbers of Servers simultaneously when in group formation. Due to the ever-variable factor of free will, both the timing and frequency of these occult summons are not fixed; they are essentially dependent upon the Server's own choices in life, and also, to a smaller degree, those made collectively by humanity.

The Servers' life-path is typically strewn with lesser and greater stimuli for awakening, especially in these final years leading up to the planetary deadline. These stimuli might be regarded as providing opportunities for initiation, yet for Servers they are but *reminders*. This is because Servers have already undergone and transcended such initiations prior to their present incarnation upon Earth. Expansions of consciousness precipitated by wake-up calls are, therefore, always familiar; in truth, they comprise an unfolding process of cumulative recall which, in turn, contributes toward the Server's training and preparation during the waiting period. As latent intelligence, knowledge and wisdom are released from within by the catalyst of wake-up calls, and as a greater degree of spiritual contact is subsequently attained, the mystery of the Server's mission is revealed to him in stages. Wake-up calls therefore help to chart the Server's path in exemplification to humanity of the fruits of the spiritual life and the way into the New World, while simultaneously they help determine his growing vision and service.

Wake-up calls can take a multitude of forms: they may present themselves spontaneously as an unexpected synchronicity in daily life; they could arise as visions, inner-plane guidance from discarnate entities or subtle senses and impressions from within; they might manifest through pictorial symbols in a piece of art or in Nature, * or perhaps in meditation or dreams; they may also be delivered in the form of

---

* For example, the crop circles are veritable wake-up calls for those who are able to recognize their symbolical meaning and significance on a deeper level than the intellect.

expressed words, either from a book, verbally or in song, or they may be received in silent recognition. They could be a welcome confirmation of a dimly sensed goal or future possibility; they might be witnessed as an incentive, a sudden inspiration or dynamic and compelling impulse in the Server's life, or they may be registered as a flash of intuitive understanding revealing a larger part of the nature of the universe. Wake-up calls will generally effect a greater appreciation of the Server's potential destiny and usefulness; they may even disclose the overall purpose of a Server's incarnation and thus stimulate a conscious aspiration toward the successful consummation of his life-mission. In whatever form wake-up calls may present themselves these precious events will reveal to the previously limited and seemingly separated consciousness of the Server at least a glimpse of the expansive, multidimensional awareness that constitutes the larger part of his own true Self, and also some small but very real sense of the existence of those transcendental worlds that are familiar territory for him.

It is usual that initial wake-up calls will begin to sound themselves spontaneously and without effort, and these may succeed in leading the Server a little way toward his goal. However, subsequent wake-up calls must be evoked by the Server's own volition. Such is an immutable law upon the True Path, and until that which has already been awarded is utilized intelligently, more will generally not be given. Revelation must always be self-engendered and may be brought about by earnest spiritual seeking and by a genuinely loving attitude. When this simple but fail-safe formula is diligently followed there will swiftly dawn within the Server's consciousness the answer to his present question, the clue to what is needed for him to move forward on his path, or certain information which, when practically applied, will reveal some doorway leading to further progress.

Wake-up calls are important events in the life of a Server for they provide testimony to vague senses that many Servers retain from their childhood, and they thereby inspire a conscious reconsecration to the noble and liberating life in service to the Divine Plan. By conferring true vision, they reveal to the Servers' awareness the ever-evolving possibilities of the spiritual life and the inevitability of the ultimate success of their collective mission. An inner certitude is thus born, and when acted upon will lead to further confirmation born of experience that is never subsequently forgotten. Depending upon the intensity of the wake-up call, the consciousness and outlook of one who has been partially awakened by it will be subtly or profoundly changed forever.

Following true wake-up calls (and not merely psychic experiences, which have become so common today), Servers will generally find it uncomfortable, if not impossible, to revert to their previous routines which shall invariably appear quite unsatisfying and bleak in light of their new and brighter perceptions. Radical changes are inevitable for each and every awakening Server in the world today as old life-patterns and ideals begin to be recognized by their expanding consciousness as inappropriate and even antagonistic to their remembered purpose in incarnation. Careers, relationships and certain mundane commitments made prior to a wake-up call will swiftly become incompatible with the new awareness being triggered from within, and past ways of living will eventually lose their appeal completely. At this time Servers may become aware that there exists a pressing need to regroup upon the physical plane, and so the greater part of their search will begin. New pathways of opportunity will then reveal themselves, leading to valuable experience that will impel Servers to resolve all disharmony in their lives in readiness for the Harvest Time. They will be compelled to face any and all fears, and to balance and clear the corresponding emotions that will arise due to the expanding new light within them.

Wake-up calls will continue to sound as long as the free will of the Server is exercised in accord with the behests of the Divine Plan; such appropriate activity is required in order to ensure that further opportunities are bestowed by the group-soul. As Servers once again consciously dedicate themselves to a worthwhile and selfless goal, a familiar spirit of consecration and unconditional love will be aroused within them. Hence, due to the dependability of their restored purity of motive and in doing their very best to meet the demands required of them, they will qualify for the receipt of greater knowledge and spiritual power that will be conferred upon them via the instrumentality of successive wake-up calls. Servers may thus begin to consciously cooperate in stimulating the rate of their own wake-up calls as they magnetically evoke new opportunities for themselves in service and thus expedite the process of remembrance.

* * *

An inspiring characteristic of early wake-up calls is that they provide a tiny yet thrilling glimpse of just how much more there is to be known and experienced upon the Server's mission. It becomes clear that there are still as yet most wonderful discoveries to be made, and although the dimly-sensed future glory remains imperceptible and incomprehensible to awakening Servers, such glimpses always beckon and inspire them onward. Servers are often awestruck and frequently overwhelmed by the light of progressively brighter revelations that pertain to the greater magnificence which awaits them beyond their presently limited but growing field of vision. Wake-up calls are therefore intended to incite further seeking and service by inspiring the Server's spiritual thirst.

Following a major wake-up call (i.e., one having significant and lasting transformative effect), Servers will generally pass through three stages of response. First comes the stage of enchantment, euphoria and of grand recognition; then a relative darkness follows, and sometimes even despair when the revelation fades, and Servers find that they must walk again in the ordinary dim shadows of the world. They now have some idea of who they are, but it is at this point that their real test lies, for they must now proceed on that inner knowledge and memory alone, and without the spiritual stimulation of the wake-up call. Moments of sometimes intense inner vision are usually balanced and integrated in this way by relatively dormant periods of reflection, absorption and consequent preparation for the next step forward. Finally, awakening Servers become so engrossed in their service, in aiding their fellows, and in helping them forward toward *their* next wake-up call, that the initial excitement and reaction are forgotten. They then discover to their surprise that at any time and at will—if it serves their selfless interests and those of the Divine Plan—the revelation and spiritual light that were first delivered by a wake-up call are forever theirs.

There are three modes of delivery for wake-up calls, which may be received either in waking consciousness or while asleep in the dream state. They are: i) a gentle, gradual and steadily unfolding process, often spanning a number of years—*the soft alarm bell*; ii) a sudden, intense and profoundly transformative awakening—*the loud alarm bell*; and iii) an overdue and startling wake-up call—*the late alarm bell*. This last kind of stimulus becomes eventually necessary due to the Server's lack of appropriate response to previous opportunities provided them, and consequently due to their failure to begin to penetrate the veil of forgetfulness in good time. The belated wake-up call will be much more demanding upon the Server due to its necessary severity. Such a sudden and intense spiritual stimulation generally presents certain hazards and may even cause damage to the lower vehicles of consciousness. As a result of this potent inflow of force the Server may be rendered mentally and emotionally unbalanced, and therefore prevented from fully completing his mission. As the planetary deadline draws nearer, such radical wake-up calls are less likely to result in positive awakenings. This is so because the needed personal purification will have been delayed for too long, and as the *Kundalini* fires are forced upwards along the spine, piercing the chakras of an impure and unprepared personality, nervous breakdown, insanity and even death may ensue. Late wake-up calls will require a very resilient constitution indeed and an unusually strong will in order for disaster to be averted. It may be clearly recognized, therefore, that there is presently an urgent need for Servers to embark upon or to swiftly proceed along the path of purification without delay.

* * *

The all-important process of awakening may be significantly accelerated by propitious meetings with other Servers of the Divine Plan. Some Servers who have yet to receive a major wake-up call may be given an opportunity to penetrate their veil of forgetfulness to some degree when another awakened individual conveys a truth to them or positively affects their consciousness by the radiation of certain auric energies. When Servers meet physically and begin to trust and open to one another, even slightly, a greater part of the group-soul is invoked. Ensuing energy-transmissions originating from the higher worlds bring light from above, as it were, and down through the lower vehicles to arrive ultimately upon the physical plane where it may heal, rejuvenate and spiritualize the bodily cells and illuminate the physical brain-consciousness. However, should such grace fail to be integrated within the personalities of Servers who are thus ministered to, and if positive change from their previous spiritual torpor is not subsequently effected by their own will, then their familiar condition of occult blindness is likely to rapidly reassert itself, and their potentially liberating vision may be lost.

Like humanity, the typically resistant egos of unawakened Servers may doubt or even react in fear and hostility as the initial stages of purification ensue resulting from wake-up calls sounded by other more awakened individuals. Thus so, in accordance with their choice to react negatively, they will voluntarily turn away from the door of opportunity as it necessarily closes in accordance with the law of free will. Depending upon various conditions, it may well be that Servers who fail to accept such grace into their lives in these critical times will not again receive a similar chance during their present incarnation, and so they shall unwittingly yet wilfully abort their mission. Those who decline opportunities to serve, and especially those who mistreat awakened Servers who endeavour to offer them help and guidance, are in danger of descending into a deep personal gloom as their own Greater Self turns away from their personality as a result of their choice to disregard a messenger of the New Spirit.

It is imperative that Servers who are still asleep and lost in ignorance should recognize other awakened Servers who may have been galvanized from within to come to their aid in answer to an earnest prayer. It should also be very well understood that when one's soul-family is beginning to reunite again upon the physical plane, it is precisely at this time that the hidden forces of selfishness will try their utmost to create apprehension, confusion, blindness and the like in all those personalities who have become infected by the pervasive distrust, fear and delusion upon Earth. There are various ways in which Servers may recognize one another, some of which have already been described, and more of these will be detailed later. However, as a general rule, Servers should learn to trust their initial feelings and perceptions (which are usually soul-born and, therefore, accurate) *before* the ego has an opportunity to becloud such valid recognition with doubt, scepticism or criticism.

* * *

The Divine Plan bears within its design special wake-up calls for a very small percentage of Servers who might be appropriately termed *early-risers*. They are awoken in advance of the majority of other Servers, and consequently they often experience much frustration, ridicule and hardship as they struggle in the darkness to learn necessary lessons by trial and error. As heralds, the early-risers are ahead of their time, and are therefore little understood and sometimes even less welcomed in a world that is not yet ready to receive them or their expanding and prophetic vision. They crow like the rooster in the darkest hour before dawn, announcing the imminent morning glory to a world that sleeps on. Even in the present stages of world preparation the task of those Servers who are charged with laying the foundations for the New Way of conscious spiritual development for mankind and with the labour of getting ready for the first awakened group members, is difficult indeed. They stand for so much that is still deemed visionary and impossible, and the formidable goals that confront early-risers may appear quite unattainable in the initial stages. However, their pioneering efforts are likely to lead to an early remembrance of who they are, together with those hard-won greater responsibilities, and will be seen to evoke their rightful reward.

Many Servers who are awoken earlier than most will find that they are compelled to resume their duty to mankind on Earth by highlighting the adjusted laws of the Aquarian age and by teaching the corresponding new truths and ways of human spiritual advancement. The initial effect of their earnest undertaking is necessarily *destructive* because they endeavour to rid mankind of all the old forms of religious, economic and political doctrine that no longer serve the world's needs. Their required impersonality— which recognizes faults as well as virtues—enrages many, even those from whom they had most expected understanding, true impartiality and collaboration. Their failure to be impressed or attentive to established rites and ceremonies, to ancient and precious yet obsolete ideas, philosophies and theologies, and their constant warfare on attachments, denials, worldly illusions and any and all obstructions to the emerging New World Consciousness, meet in the early stages with little encouragement. Early-risers work frequently alone, therefore, and usually without either support or recognition.

A very small percentage of Servers scattered around the world today are involved in the important task of dismantling the old and outmoded forms and methods (usually by exposing their flaws), while simultaneously enunciating the new principles of unity consciousness. Yet as the planetary deadline approaches and as the frequency of wake-up calls soars to meet the growing world need, their numbers are steadily increasing. They are preparing the way for the first organized bodies of Servers who, having reunited upon the physical plane in specific soul-group combinations, will proceed to assist in the next phase of the Divine Plan for Earth.

Unawakened Servers who sense the import and urgency of the call to service today but who do not yet have sure contact with their own group-soul or the divine Helpers upon the inner side of life, may benefit by taking the opportunity to utilize the wisdom and reliable guidance made available for awakening by the prescience of those early-risers who are able to see more clearly. In so doing they may avail themselves of relevant knowledge, and so, by way of the sublimation of consciousness that always accompanies new spiritual comprehension, they may expedite their own process of awakening as well as that of their fellows.

Wake-up calls are often misunderstood by Servers due to the initial excitement (emotional agitation and *glamour*), personal desire and pride which they may so easily evoke. For example, some, in their naïveté, may earnestly believe that they have suddenly and miraculously become fully enlightened, like a master of wisdom, or so divinely commissioned that they are adequately qualified to teach with spiritual authority. Such impetuous Servers would do well to ponder upon the fact that early wake-up calls herald but the beginning of a *potentially* ongoing and cumulative process of spiritual unfoldment, and that until their own tiny point of consciousness merges completely with the Cosmic Consciousness of the Universal Mind, they are at best but a messenger or servant for something much greater than their little personality.

Imprudent impulsiveness often produces much impractical idealism and delusion which, in turn, will result in a retardation of further wake-up calls, and at worst may bring about such perfect conditions within the Servers' vehicles that they become an easy target for negative psychic impression. They may then be manipulated by evil minds residing within the hidden worlds for their own sinister purposes, and it is in this way that much neutralization of the positive efforts of others is effected worldwide by well-intentioned but unwary Servers. Psychic contamination is a very common and escalating phenomena today for humanity, and may lead to outright occult possession, spelling calamity for the Server, while simultaneously fulfilling the promise of certain forebodings made thousands of years ago predicting the appearance of *"many false prophets and Christs,"* for even accomplished Servers may be misled.

Servers may also curtail their own process of awakening by their misguided use of those abilities that have been conferred upon them for the benefit of others. If the knowledge and powers given are not used wisely and selflessly in service to humanity, then the Server should expect no further wake-up calls. Indeed, should spiritual gifts be abused in service to self, great remorse may be known as the Server's privileges are quickly revoked by the groupsoul. Additionally, and due to the unwise employment of faculties that may have been stimulated by a wake-up call, imbalance is likely to ensue. This may manifest itself, for example, as a brilliant intellect but a closed heart, a distorted perception of the true Aquarian vision, or the preponderance of psychic powers, replete with all the temptations and dangers of lower psychism.

Many partially-awakened Servers, in becoming infected by the widespread glamour within the New Age movement, are today joining the swelling ranks of the enthusiastic but deceived to build fairy-tale castles in the sky. They are then proceeding with the greatest fervor to lavishly furnish their imitation *New Jerusalem* with an assorted abundance of colorful and most pleasing allurements and romantic ideals that offer little more than distractions from the real divine Work. Today, the expanding light of the New Dawn is throwing shadows in all directions; temptation is everywhere apparent, and Servers will be at a great disadvantage without basic self-knowledge and an adequate understanding of the hidden side of life.[*]

* * *

Wake-up calls sound intermittently, then, in a consecutive series of increasingly brighter realizations, and these prepare Servers to eventually receive the forthcoming conclusive Revelation—or final Wake-up Call—that will restore their full multidimensional awareness together with their higher spiritual faculties and powers as it launches them into the blissful state of divine remembrance. Upon receiving this crowning Wake-up Call, all limitations and karmic afflictions connected to the lower worlds will be completely neutralized as successful Servers emerge from their past struggles in darkness and limitation into the long-awaited majesty of their true divine estate, and as they experience their final emancipation from the world of duality and separation.

The timing of the final Wake-up Call is partially contingent upon the ongoing, invocative appeal of both Servers and humanity alike, for in a free will system divine assistance may be given only in response to sincere requests for aid. At a not-too-distant future time the crisis faced by humanity will elicit an urgent demand for effective spiritual service, and this will incite a far-reaching global invocation which, in turn, will speed up the reunification of groups of Servers as they hasten forth in response to the call of mankind and the immediate needs of the world. The concluding Wake-up Call cannot sound before the time of worldwide group reformation,

---

*   Book titles have been provided at the end of this volume in order to assist the earnest seeker in gaining such essential knowledge and understanding.

a process that is being duly expedited today. Due to the powerful synergetic dynamics evoked at that time, a profound world awakening—a global Initiation—will be catalyzed.

Servers collectively constitute a kind of living bio-spiritual orchestra, each individual or group awaiting their appropriate playing time. Prior to the occasion of their gala performance, they are necessarily silenced by the limitations imposed upon them by the veil of forgetfulness. They are, however, duty-bound to care for their instruments, keeping them in good working order, and also to keep their playing skills well honed and ready to employ. Like any professional member of an orchestra, Servers will wish to listen intently to the surrounding melody of life in patient anticipation of their wake-up calls, which will lead them to their forthcoming major cue to join in with the greater concerto. However, let it be known that today the prelude to the grand symphony of the Servers' collective mission has already begun, and the Maestro of the Divine Plan is presently summoning all the remaining members who are ready to begin playing their part.

Ultimately, those Servers who respond with sagacity and intelligent discrimination to their wake-up calls will experience valuable insight, positive expansions of consciousness, elation and expeditious spiritual unfoldment as they are much facilitated by the rising Aquarian frequencies and as they are catalyzed into a supreme awakening. They will soar to new heights of experience and expression, and they will enjoy the greatest freedom and capacity for love that they have ever known in their present incarnation. Eventually, together with the discovery of a marvellous new agility and vitality born within their finely-tuned vehicles, they will open up to a much greater inflow of spiritual force, and will finally graduate most joyfully at the impending Harvest Time, taking as many amongst humanity with them as are willing and able to rise up and behold the refulgence of the New World.

Remembrance

THE PROCESS OF REMEMBRANCE is today being hastened by those who hear, recognize and subsequently follow their soul-call, and it is these awakening individuals who are aiding in the establishment and expansion of the New World Consciousness on Earth. Upon the dawning of true understanding and subsequent obedience to the group-soul, Servers shall willingly accept the responsibility and honour of helping others spiritually. This they must do before full remembrance can be awarded them, for true spiritual Power (which is ever a distinguishing mark of divine remembrance) may only be entrusted to those who are pure in heart, and who therefore demonstrate active goodwill. By reconsecrating themselves to the furtherance of the Divine Plan, the lives of Servers will be transformed as the light and wisdom of the group-soul facilitates their awakening and consequent emergence into the very active service for which they have incarnated. In remembrance, a working knowledge of and conscious alignment with divine laws will release Servers from all identification with the imitation ego and the physical dimension of experience alone, and this will free them to become a competent light-bearer amidst the dense shadows of the world.

In the earlier stages of the recalling process, the veil of forgetfulness is usually only partially lifted and to the extent that Servers recollect but vaguely the purpose for which they have taken incarnation. However, as previously indicated, Servers with a greater recollection of their origins and an exceptional restoration of their spiritual intelligence and higher faculties may be found in the world today. Such awakened Servers are always ardently disposed to help rouse others from their long sleep, for such is a part of their remembered duty. Having acquired a sufficient realization of what lies ahead and, therefore, what will be required of them, these more aware individuals seek earnestly to impress upon others the vital reality that, without exception, only a genuinely serviceful disposition qualifies a Server to tread the True Path that leads to complete remembrance.

By maintaining a humble, seeking attitude, slumbering Servers may attract and receive help from the more awakened members of their own group-soul who are presently in incarnation, or from other Servers who are on a parallel mission, all of whom will aid them in the recalling process. Such assistance is not only available upon the physical plane, however, but can be invoked from the unseen worlds also, and this latter type of help may be received as impressions in the form of ideas and guidance from within or as direct telepathic communication from benevolent discarnate entities who reside principally upon the higher planes. These examples typify just some of the advantages that are available today, not only for Servers, but for every sincerely-invocative individual, and they are most likely to be realized when one is absorbed in some kind of serviceful activity. Bearing this in mind, Servers may become inspired to embark upon the path of conscious remembrance. They will subsequently find that their seeking and service inevitably leads them to greater understanding and illumination, and that understanding will, in its turn, naturally find its expression in renewed and dedicated service upon the ever-widening road of spiritual discovery.

* * *

Remembrance unfolds in accordance with each Server's unique karmic record and is, therefore, inseparably related to the manner in which they have lived and are today living. In their forgetfulness during this and other past physical-plane incarnations, many Servers have made certain choices motivated by fear and selfishness; they have themselves, therefore, become entangled in the global maelstrom from which they intentionally came to help liberate mankind long ago. This is because they have been unable to pierce their own veil of forgetfulness sufficiently, and have therefore blindly followed humanity in its established egotistic tendencies of self-interest, imposed by societies that have themselves remained lost for millennia in the throes of blind habit, custom and submission to very dubious but powerful authorities. Like all thinking beings, the past actions of Servers inevitably leave their mark upon the soul, and it is necessary that one's karmic scales be balanced before further spiritual progress can be made, for negative karma obstructs the light of the Spirit from irradiating the lower vehicles of consciousness, thus preventing remembrance. However, today Servers have the opportunity to swiftly release all old and deleterious karmic patterns, and this is due, in part, to the catalytic Aquarian energies that are presently engulfing planet Earth. In order to become adequately competent to assist humanity, it is essential that Servers recognize and integrate the lessons inherent within the circumstances created by their own past imprudent actions. As old tendencies rise to the surface in order to be cleared, presenting both challenge and opportunity, Servers must firmly establish anew their pledge to the group-soul that they will resist all temptation to repeat their past mistakes, and so allow no impediment to deter their resolution to help the world. This is the only way for karmically-burdened Servers to free themselves and to consequently move forward from where they are.

One popular but erroneous attitude that will almost certainly prevent remembrance, lead to much confusion and cause further struggle, is the contaminating and very narrow belief of some Servers today that nothing special need be done, and that all grace will be bestowed in good time without the need for them to make any effort whatsoever. This idea is absolutely untrue. Progress unfolds upon Earth only in accord with the law of free will, and Servers are not exempt from this law during their Earthly incarnation. If Servers remain inert, making no decisions, eliciting no action of their own volition and, therefore, allowing their will to abide in dormancy, then the Law of Recompense will remain at best neutral for them, and consequently nothing good is going to come their way. To the contrary, considering that one of the main purposes of a Server's incarnation is to show the Way by example, the opposite of beneficent reward is likely to ensue. Failure to employ free will wisely shall result in the withholding of wake-up calls and, therefore, remembrance for Servers and, as they slumber on, they will experience growing inner conflict as the Harvest Time approaches in order that they may be catalyzed into positive action in good time. In the world of a Server, inactivity is synonymous with delay and, while retarding the unfoldment of the Divine Plan, any postponement of a Server's remembrance will detrimentally affect mankind's process of awakening and liberation also; this is due to the interconnectivity of planetary consciousness.

The inertia of Servers is both their prison and their tomb, until they decide to step beyond it, and then the universe will cooperate as the following assurance from Goethe conveys:

> Until one is committed, there is hesitancy, the chance to draw back, and always ineffectiveness. Concerning all acts of initiative, there is one elementary truth, the ignorance of which kills countless ideas and splendid plans: that the moment one definitely commits oneself, then Providence moves too. All sorts of things occur to help one that would not otherwise have occurred. A whole stream of events issues from the decision, raising in one's favour all manner of unforeseen incidents and meetings and material assistance, which no one could have dreamt would have come their way. Whatever you can do or dream you can, begin it. Boldness has genius, power and magic in it. Begin it now.

It is true that mass-selfishness, fear of change, spiritual apathy and the intensifying catharsis of the world-ego, at best create a difficult environment for awakening, and thus hold back the overall grand mission of Servers. However, it is with such circumstances that Servers must learn to live and through which they must travail. Furthermore, it is precisely these problems that Servers have come to help humanity overcome, and so it may be recognized that for Servers to remain inert is to definitely neglect their voluntary responsibility to the world. Self-imposed delay is a great deal more serious for a Server than for the average person upon the spiritual path due to the important task with which they have been charged, and also because of their more advanced spiritual level; the further along the path a soul reaches, the greater its responsibility. Every moment wasted in the ignorance of self-concern is an opportunity for service lost, a chance to catalyze another Server into remembrance missed, or a helping hand withheld from humanity. When complacent Servers awaken in recollection of their purpose (either upon this side of physical death or in the astral world), they may sorely regret every precious moment that has been frittered away in their past self-orientation, for in violating the spiritual ethic of their group-soul, such lost time amounts to a failure of their voluntary duty to mankind and planet Earth.

Negative attributes of the lower self such as selfishness, sloth or pride promote spiritual blindness and hold down the vibratory rate of consciousness. Since like attracts like, such a befogged auric condition will inevitably draw in other dense etheric, astral and mental matter which, in turn, will render the lower vehicles of the Server vulnerable to influence by energies and intelligences that are much less than divine. Psychological or emotional contaminants thus attracted by Servers, particularly during their present incarnation, will at best create avoidable complications for them during their process of awakening. Beclouded Servers are unable to move from where they are until they embark earnestly and uncompromisingly upon the path of spiritual seeking. This is the first and perhaps most important step for them toward remembrance. However, it is a fact that a significant number of Servers have become so deeply entrenched in the human condition of self-obsession and spiritual lethargy upon the planet today that they may never recover in this lifetime from their amnesia. For those who have become encumbered by much additional karma since they originally volunteered to assist planet Earth numerous incarnations ago, and who are incapable or unwilling to make the right kind of effort to change, it may take many physical-plane lifetimes to reach the sufficient level of consciousness required whereby they will be able to penetrate their veil of forgetfulness, remember their origins and ancient vows, and thus continue upon their way.

* * *

Like humanity, many Servers are today spending much time, money and effort in the process of self-healing. Now, it is a fact that in order for the personality to establish spiritual contact one must be free of all psycho-emotional impediments that inevitably prevent unconditional love from being constantly expressed, and such healing is, of course, a vital requirement for all Servers who would ready themselves to receive those high-frequency energies that bring remembrance. However, **true and permanent healing cannot be effected in self-regard**, especially under the adjusted laws of the Aquarian age. For each and every Server without exception, earnest spiritual seeking and selfless service are the quickest and most fruitful ways to expedite divine remembrance and thus also personal healing. Focussing upon the lower self—the personality—with its multiple problems and delusions is definitely not the way, for *energy follows thought*, and what is focussed upon grows, particularly in these times of rapid planetary acceleration.

It is imperative that Servers establish an attitude of detachment from their personal lives. They must arrive at the understanding that their personality is but a vehicle for the group-soul—their greater self. When utilized dispassionately, the personality may serve as an instrument for the collective mind; a veritable beacon that may shine a light of Truth upon the world, soothing the ills of humanity and pioneering a new and better way of healing and spiritual advancement in the Aquarian age. Complete and permanent healing may take place instantaneously in these extraordinary times, and the new and very effective healing protocols rely upon a fundamental grasp of contemporary world conditions and requirements, basic occult understanding, an inclusive awareness (unity consciousness), and, therefore, a selflessly consecrated and so serviceful attitude. The more astute candidates for harvest are today realizing *healing through helpfulness*; they are discovering that group collaboration is especially effective in expediting such healing due to the synergetic potency made available, as the response from divine Agents upon the inner side of life—inevitable in all earnest group work—effects a greater influx of spiritual, healing energy for everyone.

Generally, and by law, when Servers are either ready to serve or to be trained for world service, members of their group will begin to appear. At this stage, Servers will have attained a sufficient degree of remembrance to be able to quickly recognize others of symbiotic vibration who, like themselves, have also incarnated from more highly evolved realms in order to offer hope, healing and salvation to humanity. When all members of the soul-family become once again naturally selfless in their present incarnation, and therefore dedicated in service to humanity, the group will be ready to fully reunite upon the physical plane, and the powerful experience of *group healing* will then be realized. It is at this time that united Servers will recognize that there is no quicker or more effective way to heal the lower vehicles of consciousness (and to thus bring about further remembrance) than by invoking the assistance of the group-soul, which is primarily concerned with *world healing*, and here is the key to success.

* * *

Today, the time has arrived for Servers to begin to realize their spiritual potential and to awaken from the limitations that the veil of forgetfulness has imposed upon them. Just a memory away stands waiting the doorway leading to the New World, and beyond it a transcendental light, a luminous aurora of untainted holiness which far surpasses the most sublime spiritual vision that may have been glimpsed during the present lifetime. Emanating from within that sentient radiance is a gently comforting, supremely loving and so, so familiar voice—yet not a voice— beckoning, softly calling all Servers to awaken, to find one another, to rise up to meet the urgent needs of a world in transition, and by helping others, to partake in the ineffable joy of divine remembrance.

As the Harvest Time draws nearer, those Servers who have managed to penetrate their veil to some degree and who have not become hopelessly incarcerated by the contagious spiritual somnambulism of the world-ego, will experience the enhancement of a very familiar delight as rising frequencies of Aquarian energy continue to irradiate their consciousness, expanding their perceptions and stimulating remembrance, bringing them ever closer to their greater spiritual awareness and immediate destiny. The veil of forgetfulness will thus be finally drawn aside completely and permanently, and Servers will enter the major reawakening phase of their present incarnation. Looking back upon the past years of their current lifetime as one recalls an old, faded memory, awakened Servers will recognize that a great deal of that life has been intelligently guided by the directives of the group mind and, having availed them of vital experience and learning, has led to their present stage of restored spiritual felicity. Consequently, in spontaneous deference to the divine intelligence of their group-soul, now tangibly *"closer than hands and feet,"* and in attuning effortlessly to the flow of intuitive wisdom and love from within, Servers will find themselves sailing upon veritable waves of grace that will propel them forward toward the New Day as they act perfectly appropriately to meet the need of each moment, in service to the world.

The process of remembrance will eventually deliver Servers to the final Great Portal that gives access to the *Inner Sanctum*: a hidden chamber which has been prepared for a momentous group-initiation that corresponds to the Great Transition and the most universally significant Harvest Time ever known upon the planet. This magnificent event will serve as a precedent for unity consciousness in the Aquarian age, and will precipitate a new era of international cooperation upon Earth. It is group love that determines the anticipated and forthcoming moment when the floodgates of divine remembrance will swing permanently open, revealing unequivocally that the Servers' past dream of loneliness, frustration and struggle has come to an end. At this time those holy forces that are still presently latent within the hearts of all Servers will be released for the uplifting, healing and blessing of the world. Such an occasion is without comparison in Earth's history, and will become a glorious reality for all those successful Servers who prepare themselves in group formation. It is at this time that all the various soul-families are destined to unite again around the world, fulfilling their ancient pledge to humanity and effecting the final consummation of the Divine Plan for planet Earth at the end of this major world cycle. All triumphant Servers will soon remember how such spiritual success and emancipation were assured them long ago by way of their selflessness during countless incarnations of service unto the *lambs of God*. On Judgement Day those who have helped to secure the liberation and ascension of the world shall claim their hard-won prize as together they enter a higher reality. This long-awaited culmination of the Servers' grand collective mission on Earth will give rise to the wondrous experience of *group remembrance,* and has been termed "The Rapture" in the New Testament.

The Personal Program

ALL SERVERS ARE EQUIPPED with what might be compared to an inner piloting device, which carries sundry directives, instructions and parameters designed to guide them upon their path in a particular way toward certain ends, like a kind of program. Such a program is personal and unique to each individual Server, and is willingly accepted by them in accord with divine consensus and practical need prior to their physical incarnation.

Among its various influences, the personal program determines the geographical location and the time of physical birth, as well as the human parents of the incarnating Server.* Astrological considerations are meticulously calculated in advance in order to institute certain patterns and events within the life of Servers whose potential for successful completion of their voluntary assignment has been foreordained. In fact, aside from karmic considerations, the major criterion that determines the Servers' eligibility for physical incarnation upon Earth is their *goal-fitness*, and their program is designed to provide repeated opportunity for success. Yet it is ever the Servers' own free will that dictates whether a favorable choice is made by them in response to life's opportunities and, therefore, whether a positive outcome is realized; the program is but a guide.

Each personal program carries privileged intelligence in the form of encoded information that is stored at various levels within the Server's psychic constitution, and collectively this information is of critical import to the unfoldment of the Divine Plan upon Earth today. Borne by a countless profusion of subtle bio-energetic nerve pathways, such data may be activated and so recalled when it is earnestly invoked, either by Servers themselves or through them by others who may seek their aid. Such invocation not only releases vital and relevant knowledge into the awareness of the Server, but also may evoke beneficent forces from higher planes

---

* Many Servers sense at a young age that, unlike their peers, for them there is an absence of the usual parental bonds. This is because it is often the case that the soul of a Server has no prior karmic link whatsoever with either the mother or father. It is quite possible that theirs is a first-time encounter, and that the parents are chosen purely for convenience, i.e., in order to provide certain conditions that may facilitate the Server's life-objective.

that will proceed to purify and uplift the consciousness of all who are involved in such a positive interchange.

The blueprints of personal programs conform to the same fundamental design for every Server: one that seeks always to impel the individual to assist in raising the planetary vibration, to sound the call to service, to respond to appeals for help, and to act as a guide for others, leading them into the New World. These, then, are the common directives of all programs. However, it may be recalled that there are diverse classes of Servers, each of whom incarnate with different parts to play within the boundaries of the Master Plan, and the unique character and expression of their roles are directly related to their particular duty, stellar or dimensional derivations, level of spiritual attainment, propensities, skills, and even the time and place at which they are born on Earth. Variations in the manifestation of the personal program are therefore multifarious. However, a basic comprehension of the general principles underlying the common structure of all programs will avail awakening Servers today of a very useful advantage that will validate and explain to them many of their idiosyncrasies, while also aiding in the process of remembrance.

The personal program provides a kind of matrix in which Servers may demonstrate the surrender of the lower self to the higher, the sublimation of the personal life into that of the divine, just as they have repeatedly demonstrated during past incarnations upon this or other worlds. However, natural laws are sometimes quite dissimilar upon different planets, being dependent upon the unique characteristics and Will of the ruling solar Deity of the system to which the planet belongs. Therefore, as exemplars of the New Way of conscious spiritual development for humanity, strategically-incarnating Servers must adjust and re-present their past wisdom, knowledge and abilities in line with current Earthly conditions, laws and needs. In this way, not only are Servers restricted by the veil of forgetfulness, but in order that they may set a perfect example to mankind, they must also become adept at relating appropriately amidst the peculiar circumstances that arise upon planet Earth, even though they may have already gained substantial levels of spiritual mastery while in dedicated service performed at other times and places.

Such necessary adjustments to their familiar and preferred way of service are often a source of consternation for awakening Servers, as their spiritual perceptions indicate unequivocally that something is gravely amiss in the way that the people of this world conduct their lives. Awakening Servers will generally regard typical Earthly existence, together with the attitudes that it engenders in the vast majority of human beings, with utter incredulity. Why should they have to wear a social mask in order to avoid misunderstanding and distrust, and to escape persecution by those whom they seek to befriend and help? Why is it necessary to tread so cautiously or to play what to them are unnatural, soul-stifling roles in order to be validated and accepted by others? Why are they so often intimidated into suppressing their natural inclinations, while consequently remaining only of very limited service to humanity when compared to their full potential? Why is it that they are prevented by society from being who they truly are, spontaneous and loving beings, free of the need or desire to censor their heartfelt expressions of what they see and know to be true? Why does mankind fail to recognize the truth offered sincerely with altruistic motives, and so decline to welcome their service with due appreciation and cooperation in order to help in effecting positive changes that are so urgently needed today worldwide? And why does there still exist such apathy and resignation in a world that has become so conspicuously sick under the present established ways of living?

As they attempt to reach out to unhappy humanity, these and other bewildering questions are prone to plague Servers, until they come to realize that insensitivity and lack of concern for the most pressing issues of the day are quite normal upon Earth: the dark planet. Indifference and other reactions born of fear and ignorance are a common result of the directives of a Server's program, which is designed to break up and to ultimately dissipate all outmoded mental constructs and inefficient systems of subsistence by introducing that which is new, good and true.

Truth is a correspondence with reality, and when words of Truth are heard by the open and receptive ear they elevate one's spirit and may even bring about permanent and positive transformation. In a world where selfishness, fear and denial predominate, however, and where the simple Truth is still an infrequent and unwelcome intruder to the barricaded hearts of so many, the bare facts may appear most threatening to those who remain attached to their illusions and who are thus unprepared to receive that which is bright, new and liberating. The impersonal Truth is anathema to the ego which for its own 'security' and comfort clings to and thrives upon falsehood. *"Men love not the light, for light reveals their wickedness; men love the dark."* —Jesus.

Negative reactions to the Servers' candor and often passionate—because urgent—appeal to humanity[*] represent an integral part of their Earthly trials. Once recognized, accepted and transcended by applying detached wisdom, however, such trials will serve to instruct and temper the awakening soul, yielding positive and useful experience, and sometimes even invoking beneficent forces into the world that on some level *will* be received and greatly appreciated by mankind.

* * *

"There are a thousand hacking at the branches of evil, to one who is striking at the root." — Henry Thoreau.

Unlike most people in the medical and caring professions today, the more advanced Servers are not solely interested in patching up those wounds which are repeatedly self-inflicted due to ignorance; they have not incarnated merely in order to offer *band-aids* and commiserations for humanity's suffering. Servers are here today to uproot the underlying *causes* of mankind's afflictions, and to thereby effect permanent healing worldwide. Yet the great dragons of custom and conformity continually thwart their efforts to introduce anything new and unorthodox, even if tangible proof of its efficacy is offered, and so it is often the case that Servers are coerced by society to compromise upon their real service-potential. Such attitudes at best seek only to incarcerate Servers within the mediocrity of 'normal life'; misery loves company, as does ignorance. However, it is quite impossible for Servers to compromise themselves without experiencing undesirable repercussions, for their program will compel them to live in accord with what they feel and

---

*   There exist certain parameters within a Server's personal program that sometimes act like a kind of safety valve, and mental blocks may occasionally be experienced when attempting to share too much information of a sensitive nature at the wrong time or with the wrong person. Divine intervention is instant and will always prevent too grave a mistake from being made by the over-zealous personality of a Server. However, should the Server continue in their attempts to be of assistance to those who really do not wish to be or who simply cannot be helped, they may find that they become enervated or confused, clearly indicating that they are doing something wrong.

know. Consequently, in ultimately refusing to conform to certain established yet outdated and inefficient methods, Servers find that they regularly evoke disdain from those who are steeped in tradition and limited thinking. Some Servers may even be persecuted in their own homes and by their colleagues. Others, as a result of humanity's rebuttal of them and their unfolding program, may necessarily recede into the background of society, and may therefore appear to be less active outwardly, and so again be misjudged. Yet to those Servers who have achieved some remembrance of who they are and, therefore, a measure of comprehension of their program as it relates to human life on Earth, none of this will matter; their way is clear, their terms of service are known to them, and their spiritual understanding, conviction and vision will continue to grow in readiness for the Harvest Time.

It is a fact that the closer one gets to one's spiritual goal, the steeper becomes the path leading to the mountain top, and the more insurmountable will life's obstacles at first appear. Such signs illustrate progress and are inevitable; they constitute an important aspect of the Law of Karma. Spiritual progress indicates greater readiness to resolve past karma and to pass more challenging trials for the sake of speedier spiritual advancement, and divine Agents will see to it that karma is apportioned to each soul perfectly appropriately in order that it may be balanced at the earliest and safest opportunity. To the esoterically-aware, therefore, difficulties and challenges along life's road are recognized for what they really are: benevolent opportunities, and are thus happily welcomed (even if sometimes only after the event!).

An elementary understanding of universal law, the state of the world and the prudent acceptance of apparent personal injustices will avail Servers of necessary detachment in the face of all derision and rejection. They may then review their life-patterns and experiences impersonally, and thereby recognize and learn well the lessons afforded them by their program. It is so easily forgotten upon Earth that Love and Intelligence pervade the entire universe; absolutely everything in Creation is sustained and overseen by divine fiat: *"… not one tiny sparrow falls to the ground without thy Father's knowledge."*—Matt. 10:29. Therefore if pain or struggle are known at all, and if afflicted Servers wish to learn and so obviate future educational hardships, they should seek to uncover the important lesson that is always nested within their reaction to life's spiritual opportunities. Lessons learned by Servers courtesy of their program will presently synthesize themselves into greater empathy and compassion for humanity and Earthly life. Thus, the Server progresses, and the corresponding divine premiums are certain.

Insightful and informed, then, Servers will continue to be motivated to initiate a sincere and spiritually-invocative attitude in all areas of their lives, and this will allow them to progressively sense the reality of their guiding program, and to consequently harmonize their consciousness with the great Law of Service to which the group-soul naturally pays obeisance. By responding spiritually and, therefore, appropriately to the invariable opportunities that the tensions of the world provide, Servers are sure to receive the incoming new energies that are available to them and so may begin to consciously manifest the purpose of their incarnation by exemplifying the way of attunement to the new and adjusted laws of the Aquarian age.

Cumulative revelation and remembrance will inevitably be experienced by Servers as they pierce the veil of forgetfulness by living progressively more in accord with their program and preordained mission. This they do by *acting* appropriately instead of *reacting* blindly. Guidance along such worthwhile lines has been offered by the countless sages, wise thinkers and true spiritual teachers throughout Earth's history,* yet unawakened Servers, like the majority of human beings, have not generally trusted themselves or the universe enough to apply those very simple principles that would allow them to live by life's grace as all the saints have done. TRUST—not fear—is indeed an all-important key to success in these times, and when Servers begin to listen well and continually to their own *inner teacher*, resisting the influence of the typically fallacious opinions belonging to others who are themselves so often lost in error, they shall instigate a simple yet powerful process that will guide them unerringly forward along the Lighted Way.

* * *

During the waiting period Servers sometimes embody and demonstrate the opposite characteristics to those which they will express once they awaken, and such polarization is an important aspect of their program. Limited by both the veil of forgetfulness and by certain necessary restrictions inherent within the personal

---

*   Krishna, Lord Buddha, Jesus and all the truly Great Servers throughout religious history succeeded in following the behests of their own personal programs to perfection.

program, Earthly existence is so often a source of much anxiety for Servers, who may, nevertheless, eventually and completely transcend every shortcoming, weakness and need of the lower self in order to exemplify success and mastery in a particular sphere of human achievement. It may be remembered that Servers incarnate to play the drama of human life at all levels, and they are ultimately destined to reawaken later into the relative perfection of their true Nature, and to realize that their temporary roles as, for example, criminals, prostitutes, tramps, etc., were assumed as a part of their program so that they could experience, learn, transmute and thus serve at that level.

As has been mentioned previously, under the direction of the group mind and during the earlier stages of their unfolding program, Servers collectively demonstrate all human patterns of dysfunction. The pain and inner conflict that such afflictions engender is never forgotten and necessarily draws upon the resources of the heart. These disharmonious patterns thus provide the needed crisis-points for Servers whereby they may ultimately learn to master certain aspects of the human condition. It is often the case that in the earlier stages the personal program proves to be rather stringent indeed, yet awakening Servers will always be compelled to sublimate the negative elements of their program into their corresponding positive, creative expression. In thus emerging triumphantly from the dysfunctional human experience, accomplished Servers will ultimately express, while in physical embodiment, certain unique aspects of the group-soul that are permitted by the parameters of their program. Once their trials have been overcome, duly evoking greater confidence, remembrance and illumination, Servers will be able to enter the next stage of their progressively-unfolding program, and will hence be qualified to lead humanity from darkness into light.

Should Servers fail to move forward upon their path by repudiating the 'legitimate suffering' of the human experience, perhaps by anesthetizing themselves in an endless search for distraction and self-gratification, and should they thus stray from the intended designs of their program, they will find that ever greater difficulties will arise in their lives, and much more so than is normal as a result of the shortcomings of the average human being. Imprudent attitudes and reactions to the challenges elicited by the personal program may create grave problems for a Server and exemplify to humanity how *not* to behave upon the eve of the New Day. However, even such avoidable ordeals will yield their own particular benefit in the long-run despite their typically more painful nature, for they are actually necessary lessons effected by contingency parameters within the personal program in order to encourage Servers to resume their journey upon the straight and narrow path.

When a Server has recognized the wisdom of paying attention to and trusting their own program, they will find that they are provided with an infallible source of spiritual guidance that will lead them safely (even if not entirely unscathed!) through all their Earthly trials. A recognition of the whispered messages of the personal program can be assured by understanding and retaining one very elementary fact in these critical times: a Server's state of consciousness will rise when acting in alignment with the Divine Plan, or deteriorate when doing something that is detrimental to the greater good, and thus unfavorable for the Server also. When such subtle inner guidance is ignored, the group-soul will always recede, and this may result in gloomy depressions, despondency, spiritual anguish and the like, all of which are sure indications that the Server is contravening his program.

If Servers sense that something is amiss in their life; if, for example, they experience inexplicable sombre moods, then there is certainly an important lesson that is trying to reach their conscious awareness, courtesy of their program, and which is waiting to be duly recognized in order that they may proceed from where they are. Upon their Earthly mission, and no matter how thick the veil of forgetfulness, the group-soul speaks perpetually to Servers through absolutely everything: Nature, people, dreams, feelings, moods, common events, etc., and always with the one sole objective to be of assistance. Should Servers maintain a mindful awareness during these final years preceding the Harvest Time, they will be able to recognize certain vital hints that occur in their lives, and which are afforded them by the relatively omniscient spiritual intelligence of the group mind. Should Servers follow well the behests of their own program they will know progressive positive impetus, clarity and spiritual upliftment together with that joy which ever accompanies divine purpose. The delight of beholding Nature speaking as she reveals her secrets in a steady flow of harmonious synchronicity is but one reward bequeathed to Servers once they (re-)learn how to trust and follow the stream of grace available from within.

Servers would do well, therefore, to wholeheartedly follow their own inner guide—their personal program—as best they can, even if that guidance leads them through trials that may at first appear quite formidable, irrational or perhaps entirely insurmountable.

With their gaze fixed one-pointedly upon the road ahead, they may confidently walk the True Path that leads to victory and Liberation, remembering always the biblical proposition: *"Though I walk through the valley of the shadow of death, I shall fear no evil."* Servers' ordeals are designed to ultimately release the transmuting power of wisdom within them, and so enrich the world. In triumphantly radiating the light of transformation, awakening Servers affect not only those who are exposed to their auric field, but also sow seeds of a new and higher vibration into the subtle energy grid of the planet, thereby making it easier for all humanity to make the journey into the New World.

* * *

It should be mentioned that Servers will generally find that traditional spiritual practises fail to yield the results that are indicated by the various teachings and textbooks, and this is due to the *timing element* within their program. For example, a Server may practise meditation for twelve hours a day over a ten year period or more but with little effect when compared to the great yogis and mystics of yore, for the group-soul will not allow them individually to push past a certain level of awareness or spiritual attainment in their present incarnation before the appropriate time.

Spiritual exercises, such as meditation, are not employed by Servers in the same way as they have been by mankind generally down through the ages. Awakened Servers know that their spiritual practises are performed solely for the training and upkeep of the etheric, emotional and mental bodies. It is these lower vehicles of consciousness—created anew in each corporeal incarnation as is the physical body—that are to be matured, and not the soul of the Server. Actually, a Server's already spiritually advanced group-soul naturally meditates upon its own plane as it simultaneously works and serves, and effects of this sometimes filter down into the Server's waking consciousness causing spontaneous, profound and seemingly unprovoked spiritual senses and experiences, although such activities of the group-soul need not synchronize with that of the Server's personality.

Meditation and the like should therefore be regarded by Servers as *spiritual maintenance* rather than a means to attain a new goal, one that has, in fact, already been achieved by them on the other side of the veil of forgetfulness. It is sometimes the case that meditating Servers attain a somewhat surprising level of inner harmony and joy rather quickly during the early stages of spiritual practise while in Earthly incarnation, yet only to be thrown out of their peaceful state by the group-soul with the stark reminder of the suffering in the world, and the subtle reprimand that they have not incarnated for their own sake. If, however, the Server meditates with the sincere attitude of doing so *for others*, the group-soul will remain acquiescent and may even confer blessings in various ways. Such is the essential difference between the meditator of the past who typically sought after self-liberation, and that of today who, if they practise at all, must practise for others in order to receive the Aquarian grace and subsequently embody the New World Consciousness.

* * *

When the initial phases of a Server's program have been successfully accomplished due to wise commitment and corresponding action, the general directives of the intermediate stages will readily evince themselves. Provided Servers continue to follow their assignment, fulfilling their duty with entirely selfless motives, previously inhibited higher psychic faculties and spiritual awareness will begin to be restored. Their ability to wield the secret forces of Nature will again be elicited, and so their greater function as divine agents upon Earth shall once again be evidenced by them.

At this stage, Servers may begin to work occultly upon the hidden side of life. They will become aware that by invoking certain beneficent forces into the world they are able to produce life-enhancing energy-currents and thought-forms upon those higher planes that are today unpopulated by humanity's predominantly dense mental and emotional projections. Elevated spiritual vibrations—being much more subtle and penetrating than are the more gross vibratory energies generally produced by mankind—have a much greater longevity and far wider field of influence for conferring blessings and bestowing healing in the world. Additionally, the higher frequencies that characterize the consciousness of all awakened Servers positively affect the subtle energy fields of the Earth in readiness for the time when humanity's own consciousness ascends, and is therefore able to attune to and benefit from those spheres that will have been prepared for them. The creation of positive etheric, astral and mental energies is a most valuable service indeed, and such silent esoteric work constitutes a vital part of a Server's world duty.

Awakening Servers may be encouraged to know that the enhancement and strengthening of that great reservoir of spiritual force to which they automatically contribute by way of their benevolent nature and activity may represent their greatest service prior to the final Wake-up Call at the Harvest Time, and is, in part and of itself, a fulfilment of their program. Servers lacking recollection of occult law may fail to appreciate that while the immediate effects of esoteric work—conscious or subconscious—may go unnoticed by most, the genuine and most productive causes instigated by the radiation of positive energies conferred upon higher and more subtly-efficacious planes will continue to reverberate throughout the spheres of planet Earth for generations to come, blessing and awakening even those who have no particular disposition toward spiritual good. A Server's unseen metaphysical activity is actually one of the highest forms of occult meditation; one which has ever been practised by every agent of the Divine Plan throughout cosmic history. The hidden side of this kind of service may be appreciated, then, as being of significant cumulative value, and such worthwhile accomplishments constitute a vital part of the overall positive effects that may be rendered by following the directives of the personal program.

The Group Program

THE TYPICAL LIFE UPON EARTH for most people in our modern times may be compared to a mighty labyrinth, replete with challenges, riddles to solve, decisions necessitated regarding which direction to take, and hopefully the unearthing of a treasure or clue from time to time that may help the adventurer along his way. Like most puzzles of its kind, the labyrinth of life invariably contains a most valuable prize that rests at the centre of the maze, and it is this very location toward which everyone is headed, whether they realize it consciously or not.

The lives of Servers who are lost in the labyrinth of Earthly experience are no exception to this general pattern, and they are also attempting to arrive at the centre, though very often in their forgetfulness they may fail to realize exactly what they are seeking, let alone where it lies. Their personal program dutifully urges them toward their ultimate destination by gentle suggestion and by subtle hints along the way. Whether they opt to follow the sure guidance of their inner Shepherd or not, the group-soul endeavours unceasingly to inspire them forward upon the True Path in order that they may discover in good time all the appropriate clues, keys and other articles that are essential to the success of their mission.

Upon their gruelling quest, candidates for glory must strive to locate the vitally-required *Golden Thread*, which is guaranteed to guide them forth unerringly through many a dragon's lair en route to the centre. Amongst the numerous items of use to be found along the way is the *Scrying Crystal of Far-Seeing*, which shall prove to be an indispensable aid in progressively revealing to them the secrets of the labyrinth as well as divulging essential hints to the mystery of their assignment. By employing such a precious find wisely and faithfully they will be able to pass safely through all the doors and passageways that lead eventually to the great *Gates of Fortune*. This final portal will at last deliver the wearied aspirant to the *Sacred Vault* at the heart of the intricate maze where the priceless *Jewel of Remembrance* awaits his rightful claim.

The Servers' prize is indeed a great trophy worthy of seeking because, once located, it will lift them into unprecedented regions of expanded spiritual awareness. However, those splendid treasures to be gained in the typical fantasy-adventure are never won easily; to be so would simply present no challenge to the brave hero or heroine in the narrative. The story of the Path of Liberation is the same, and where there is tension, struggle or difficulty of some kind, then it is certain that within such an ordeal lies opportunity for a new discovery and, therefore, progress. Thus so, Servers should not expect to find the philosopher's stone without effort, yet it ought to be remembered that the quest itself is a very important part of their unfolding program; a symphony ought to be enjoyed in its entirety, and not merely in anticipation of its grand finale.

The dense vibratory regions of the Earth-labyrinth invariably present a multitude of formidable obstacles and trials, and consequently some Servers may become hopelessly lost amidst its tortuous network of tunnels and passages...or almost, for there are certain provisions made in every Server's program in the event of emergency. Staying with our analogy, there will doubtlessly be other more successful adventurers who have come closer to prevailing over the enigmatic maze, and who may have even victoriously retrieved their personal prize at its centre. Help is at hand courtesy of these accomplished Servers who will have: i) pierced to some degree their veil of forgetfulness; ii) accessed the corresponding phase of their own program; iii) restored a greater level of remembrance than those who are still perplexed and wandering alone in the labyrinth; and iv) consequently recognized their fellow seekers and begun to advance their collective mission by uniting with their soul-group on the physical plane.

As the personal program unfolds, it is clearly recognized to be just a small but integral part of a larger and much more important *group program*, the success of which may be known only in association with others. Consequently, those Servers who have succeeded in reaching the centre earlier than most, will subsequently proceed back into the labyrinth in order to find other bewildered seekers and guide them along the correct path. Awakened Servers will thus lead those who are tarrying behind them upwards from the great underground catacombs of their past trials, directing them forward beyond their previous limitations in darkness and confusion, and ultimately out of the labyrinth and into the light of the New World.

* * *

To begin with, then, Servers primarily seek out clues to their own personal programs, individually and alone, yet they are very likely to meet with one another at certain times along the way as their paths cross. When two or more members of the same or kindred soul-groups convene, there is almost always an instinctive recognition on some level, which may be evidenced in numerous ways. Examples may include: witnessing the Law of Synchronicity in action as it manifests curious and magical 'coincidences' in connection with the encounter; a flash recall, a vague memory of a previous incarnation together and a warm feeling of familiarity; a sudden sensing of a similarity of vision and of life-objective; or an instantaneous electrical interplay, often experienced as a thrilling, tingling sensation in the area of the heart or head and throughout the body. Should this last dynamic be allowed to run its course, it may facilitate a major wake-up call by vivifying the aura of each Server and thereby stimulating their consciousness. A circuit of metaphysical force may be effortlessly set up in this way, and the elation conferred by such a phenomenon may be regarded as an unparalleled experience of grace by those who are affected, yet during the waiting period such a trickle of the New World Consciousness is actually but a tiny indication of far greater things to come.

By piercing the veil of forgetfulness to some degree and in thus recalling the purpose of their incarnation, Servers naturally become catalysts for one another's further advancement toward the light of remembrance. All Servers who begin to awaken become capable of stimulating other receptive Servers into recognition of their own personal programs as well as the greater group duty. Due to the expanding and unifying awareness of Servers all around the planet today the *group catalyst* is beginning to be activated, the synergetic potency of which shall significantly contribute toward liberating harvestable humanity. The potential of this group catalyst is related to the harmonious fusion of the diverse but complementary characteristics expressed by each individual Server. In order for success to be known, the assets and qualities of each Server must be consecrated to the good of the group, to humanity and to the world. Servers must find one another and work together again as one unified body in their present incarnation; to remain isolated is to opt to take no part in the most important aspect of their collective mission: the group program.

Upon meeting and recognizing each other, awakened Servers will know at once that their ultimate goals are identical, and they will be subsequently impelled to collaborate in order to ascertain where teamwork and supplementary endeavour may be possible for the furtherance of the One Work. However, it should be understood that group work proceeds unimpeded within the higher worlds where purposeful union and intelligent service are ever spontaneous and constant. Therefore, physical proximity is not necessary for group collaboration to be effected within the inner spheres of the planet by the Servers' higher consciousness. Yet, an initial terrestrial encounter will often serve to facilitate cooperation upon the hidden side of life by way of the Servers' self-generated thought-forms of one another. Such thought-forms, produced voluntarily in mental and astral matter, are then able to be utilized for communication and contact upon the corresponding planes by the souls with whom they are identified, and it is thus that occult group work may continue during the waiting period without the need for further physical association.

As important and integral parts of the group program, timely rendezvous upon the physical plane are designed to function as a stimulus for further insight, understanding and remembrance. They also serve to demonstrate the advantages of and essential requirements for group contact during the waiting period. Such encounters are scheduled by the group-soul but most often remain unknown to the Servers' waking consciousness, and are, therefore, usually completely unanticipated by them. These predestined appointments along life's pathways are opportunities for Servers to confer with one another in order to exchange important key information, and to transmit and receive complementary energies. Purposefully designed and intelligently regulated, the manifestation upon the physical plane of such synchronistic meetings in the lives of Servers demonstrates just one aspect of the overall directives of the group mind; they are essential components of the larger plan, which has been carefully designed by that great collective awareness that is itself responsible for implementing and overseeing the group program, as well as skillfully guiding it toward the destined accomplishment of its goal.

* * *

Servers who have recalled something of their duty upon Earth will naturally wish to help prepare the way for others, and it is the responsibility of the more awakened individuals to alert those who may still be faltering within the labyrinth to the all-important existence of the collective mission. In order for collaboration to then commence without delay, it is important for Servers to join forces in wholehearted dedication to the highest good of which, as a group, they have become aware. Three major virtues will be essentially required by each and every individual who wishes to join such a valuable alliance today, and these will be vital to the restoration of complete remembrance and, therefore, group success. These virtues are: i) a basic comprehension of the design and aim of the overall Divine Plan at this juncture of human development; ii) a genuine willingness to achieve perfect alignment with the orientation and purpose of the group program as determined by the group members; and iii) a consequent throwing of the total of one's resources into the furtherance of the immediate divine objective for humanity and planet Earth via the instrumentality of the group.

Should the solidarity aspect of the group program fail to be realized and demonstrated, then such untapped potential will necessarily prevent Servers from actualizing their full spiritual capacity as a cohesive unit, unity consciousness will reside in dormancy, and the greatest triumph, the sweetest victory—known only in fulfilment of the ultimate objective of the group program—will consequently remain out of reach.

The call to world service is today being trumpeted in the ear of every able-bodied man and woman on Earth. All soul-families are presently being invited to reunite upon the physical plane, and this inevitable regrouping process is now underway worldwide. Spirited motivation for group collaboration and joint service by awakening Servers will naturally follow their recognition of the world's dire need, a realization of the existence of the Divine Plan, an apprehension of the immediate point of mankind's attainment and, therefore, an insight into world potential. Subsequent to such discernment, the Aquarian age way of conscious spiritual development through collective service will be exemplified by Servers; a path that has for ages been dutifully followed predominantly upon the hidden side of life by Earth's own planetary Hierarchy which has happily progressed while aiding and protecting its younger brothers and sisters: humanity.

Mankind's readiness today to step forward onto a higher turn of the evolutionary spiral—the path of group spiritual growth—is a very positive sign indeed, for it reflects an important and inevitable universal process whereby individuality merges back into the Oneness of the Divine. Such unification is the ultimate goal of all sentient beings within every sphere of Creation, and it is this one great objective toward which the driving thrust of the divine Spirit eternally urges all suffering life.

*   *   *

Upon their Earthly sojourn all Servers must initially venture forth upon a lonely path, separated from their soul-family and isolated in their search for Life and Purpose. During their quest for remembrance they will naturally seek to share something of the Truth which they have recalled so far, and to offer that understanding which is theirs to others wherever they may find themselves and in whatever capacity they labour. Individually, their task may seem small, but collectively they form a very substantial global latticework of spiritual light, forged today in readiness for the physical manifestation of *Light Centres* all around the planet.

Upon the subtle planes each individualized Server stands behind and supports the other, awaiting eventual reunification and subsequent group remembrance upon the physical plane where the culminating majesty of the group program will be realized. Today, as the planetary deadline draws swiftly closer, many of those who have worked during the past in relative seclusion are consciously seeking to unite with kindred souls in order that group synergy may be potentiated and so that the great ethereal web of light—now woven around the globe and interpenetrating it—may be vitalized to its highest capacity and its potencies thenceforth released upon the physical plane where they will ultimately proceed invincibly to effect the necessary, long-overdue and complete healing of planet Earth together with all life thereupon.

It should be understood that, contrary to popular belief and during the transition period, those Light Centres having the most far-reaching and beneficent influence will not be primarily healing centres; they will be centres of spiritual service bearing many different functions, only one of which shall be personal healing. It is the responsibility of genuine spiritual communities to offer a field of service to those who wish to help raise the planetary consciousness by purifying their own. Selfless service, in raising the vibratory rate of consciousness, induces a process of transmutation and necessarily confers comprehensive healing, yet does not focus solely upon it, and this is a vital key to success during the birth of the New World. Healing is an integral part of any truly divine work, but should it be the prime focus of any community, then such a group will be extremely limited from the start, for there is something of far greater moment than personal healing and happiness, and which is today calling humanity from divine spheres.

Following the efficient, logical framework exemplified by all successful esoteric schools of the past, the occult structure of Light Centres in the Aquarian age will incorporate inner and outer circles. These concentric rings of serviceful activity will reflect the degree of spiritual attainment and, therefore, capabilities of those souls who work within their boundaries. In accordance with their own abilities, level of commitment, purity of motive, point of spiritual attainment and merit, aspirants will be naturally drawn inwards toward those groups who demonstrate greater spiritual influence and responsibility. Each person will find the appropriate position or office that will present the best opportunities for them, while simultaneously harmonizing with the collective purpose and, therefore, the good of the whole group.

* * *

Much more important, then, than the personal program is the group program, yet greater even than the group program is the Global Agenda, which embraces the sum total of all efforts made by the multifarious assemblages of Servers—both physically incarnated and incorporeal—who will together usher in the New World Consciousness on Earth and thus assist in preparing humanity for the birth of the New Eden for planet Earth. The Global Agenda is no less than the invincible Divine Plan for humanity and the planet itself, and the exultant fanfares of its prophesied and long-awaited triumph for this current phase of solar evolution will be heard by all mankind soon after the required critical mass has been gathered together under the auspicious guidance of the Servers. Strategically-placed *nodes of light* (comprising many souls who have aligned themselves with the Divine Will in holy service) will then begin to expand, linking-up around the world via the Earth's subtle energy grid to form one great sphere of loving force that will be responsible for launching the whole planet into a higher reality.

The essential nature of the group program may be regarded esoterically as a great and sovereign Thought that was conceived within the Mind of God at the beginning of Creation, and which has since been constantly expanding and developing. This Cosmic Idea is an integral part of the Universal Divine Plan of Evolution for all life throughout Infinity. Its particular form of expression, as it influences our world, is ever being adjusted to integrate appropriately with the current cycle of development so that it may correspond with and assist the specific level of consciousness demonstrated by humanity at its particular stage of spiritual unfoldment.

Forever, the group program has manifested itself as an intelligent and purposeful evolutionary pattern incorporating great complementary Forces that have progressively advanced themselves throughout innumerable incarnations in a multitude of different worlds. Originating from diverse realms in all parts of the Cosmos, these consciously-evolving Forces are ensouled within the lower spheres of the universe by a myriad of both collective and singular embodiments. Karmically related each to the other, these temporarily individualized and differentiated lives are naturally impelled to coalesce and separate repeatedly during innumerable interdimensional transmigrations of intentional service across vast regions of space and eons of time.

Each seemingly separate life knows that it is essentially an indivisible part of the Whole, and that in synergetic union far greater achievements may be realized than by the sum efforts of the individual parts alone. Cosmic law greatly favours the cumulative and selflessly-directed attention of a group of dedicated souls who are able to work together as one. When pure motives for loving service are foremost, unity consciousness draws upon an insuperable Power that ever bestows the assurance of success, and the group program has always as its indomitable motivating thrust the sole determination to fulfil perfectly the behests of the Divine Plan. Therefore, absolutely nothing in the whole of Creation can prevent the inevitable triumph of the group program.

A brief, mystical analogy may here serve to offer just a hint of the complex dynamics that are initiated within the higher worlds when awakened Servers begin to reunite for group work upon the physical plane. Each individualized fragment of the group-soul and its personality (the Server) bears a unique musical chord. Timing is of the essence, and when the soul-family regroups once again at the appointed hour upon Earth, each individual tone will combine to produce a transcendental code that will be peculiar to the group, and which will confer certain occult privileges. When the correct number and combination of notes are sounded together synchronously, a secret latch will be triggered, a hidden portal will be opened, and a great Mystery shall be revealed.

It is thus that the overall collective mission of Servers upon Earth might be compared to a great symphony comprising many and diverse musical notes. Yet if one or more within the planetary orchestra ventured to play their instrument too early and before time, a dissonance would be heard, a confusion would eventuate amongst all the players, the medley would fracture, and the world auditorium would be thrown into disharmony with the Divine Plan. For the global symphony proper cannot really begin before a certain stage of world preparedness. However, let all awakening

Servers and readied humanity alike now be assured that they are about to commence playing the most beautiful and melodious part of the Great Rhapsody in which all Earth-life has been waiting to partake since mankind's *fall from Paradise.*

The Portal to the New World

DEDICATED GROUPS are today making contact with divine Intelligence upon the inner side of life with the sole intention of uniting in holy service for the greatest possible good. Thus so, certain spiritual forces are made available and are facilitating the dissolution of all personal concerns in the joy, security and purpose of group communion, while simultaneously opening an invisible channel within the centre of the group through which these forces may flow. Inevitably, grace streams forth via the higher planes and through such purposefully-constructed conduits of spiritual blessing, thereby illuminating the consciousness and opening the hearts of those present. Such a process catalyses the rapid transmutation of all gross auric energies, thereby releasing personal psycho-emotional blockages and producing various healing wonders as it leads to emancipation from all worldly pain and suffering. The unselfish and intelligent use of such a powerful method of conducting divine energy in these favorable times gives rise to the construction of a potent ethereal circuit that blazes a stream of electric force through every opened heart and bestows Revelation upon the whole group as each individual's consciousness fuses and unites with the group mind and is subsequently lifted into luminous spiritual realms where the experience of unconditional love for everyone and everything is known. Thus are portals to the hidden worlds opened and traversed.

Yet this is not all; indeed, it is only the beginning, for in employing the Law of Invocation synergetically within the group, the corresponding influx of divine force not only uplifts and sanctifies the consciousness of those responsible for its induction, but then proceeds to radiate outwards from the centre, simultaneously effecting the transmutation of negative energies in the surrounding environment by purifying, healing and vivifying all the kingdoms of life on Earth: mineral, vegetable, animal and, of course, human. Such auspicious activity today is, in part, responsible for the summoning, anchoring and worldwide distribution of the new Aquarian frequencies of light-energy. These new energies are preparing the way for the descent of the Christ-Consciousness in many by fostering the emergence of the spiritual human being upon the planet, and are thus contributing toward the establishment of the *"Kingdom of God"* on Earth.

The manifestation of metaphysical portals may be greatly facilitated by the positive influence of certain Earth-energies, and havens for refuge, healing and preparation are being established by Servers around existing Earth-vortexes upon the physical plane in readiness to be used as portals for consciousness to travel into the higher worlds. These havens are destined to become veritable beacons of light due to the intense spiritual activity which they will engender. Awakened Servers are being attracted to assist in the construction and consecration of such 'arks' which, among many other things, will offer the needed protection from the 'global flood' that is now imminent. Amongst the ranks of such Servers, those who have integrated unity consciousness into their lives will act as gatekeepers of the portals, and will thereby fulfil the ultimate part of their function as harvesters.

As the Piscean age draws to a close, those who have adequately raised their vibratory rate of consciousness by responding positively to world need and, therefore, by serving humanity together in groups, will have the opportunity to pass through the Portal of Initiation prior to the major planetary Initiation itself. Other servants of the race will be able to follow later as they are duly honoured, rewarded and liberated at a time that is in alignment with their personal and group programs, and to a level that is in direct proportion to the degree to which they have given of themselves in selfless service over numerous incarnations.

It should be understood that the Portal of Initiation leading to the New World may only be traversed in group formation; such is a law of the Aquarian age. All those accomplished candidates for ascension will assemble on this side of the portal, as it were, and once the group conduit has been opened by righteous and timely invocation, a flood of Servers will pour through. Upon the inner side, these triumphant individuals will behold a 'stairway of light' spiralling forth from the mundane realms of the physical plane. This endless stair will be very familiar to all Servers, extending ever-upward and disappearing from sight as it merges into fathomless brilliance above. The border of these ethereal steps will be lined with deceased loved ones, angelic guides, prophets and saintly personalities of past Earthly accomplishment and renown, together with a myriad miscellany of curiously familiar divine Agents from other lofty civilizations who will be waiting in readiness to assist all those worthy souls along the way, as well as to share in the spiritual merit harvested from Earth by the Servers. A momentous greeting and most loving reception indeed awaits those who achieve what they originally set out to do by passing a long and stringent test spanning lifetimes of trials. All is balanced and rewarded perfectly by divine Order at the Harvest Time.

Via a profusion of intentionally-opened portals around the planet, there will occur multiple ascensions of groups of Servers preceding multiple *resurrections*, when many will return to Earth etherealized and functioning in full multidimensional consciousness. This phenomenon will continue up until the moment of the final Great Transition, which shall *seal the door where evil dwells*, and so liberate humanity on Earth. Such is graduating mankind's predestined fortune—or *Deliverance*—spoken of in diverse prophecies and found in numerous scriptures of old. Together, then, successful Servers and those amongst humanity who have prepared themselves adequately will progress through levels of group unification as they experience numerous lesser initiations in preparation for the great global Initiation that will escort them all through the Portal and into the New World.

✳ ✳ ✳

Once the planetary deadline has arrived, many Servers will have successfully completed their task of ushering Earth into the new cycle and they will no longer choose to remain within the planetary sphere during the succeeding transitions. For these accomplished Servers, Judgement Day will represent an invitation for them to return to their familiar home-density, and, for some, to venture beyond it. Others, even those in close proximity and who may have collaborated personally with the first wave of returning Servers, will not yet leave Gaia; their group program will inspire them to continue in their service of building the New World on Earth during the Aquarian age together with humanity.

At the Harvest Time, those successful Servers who have chosen to leave the Earth spheres will ascend through various worlds and densities on their homeward journey. Having previously reunited with numerous other incarnations of their group-soul upon the physical plane in order to realize together the consummation of the terrestrial element of their grand mission, the most evolved Servers will pass up from third-density Earthly experience in group formation and through the fourth and fifth densities as they are greeted with unprecedented veneration and praise by legions of Celestial Hosts within the unseen worlds, and as they partake in the ineffable glories of the long-promised Great Rejoicing. Continuing onward and upward through the Christed frequency (the sixth density), they will journey on into the seventh sphere: the *Buddha realms*, where the most exalted Lives within our Cosmic Physical Plane are waiting to move up into the next Octave of evolutionary experience: *the Cosmic Astral Plane*, an unplumbed region of Infinity where a bright new chapter in the Story of Creation is about to begin.

The reality of such a triumphant return is supernally metaphysical and subtle beyond utterance; the divine reward and supreme exultation awaiting those successful Servers who will once again become transfigured and absorbed into the transcendental refulgence of one perfectly united spiritual consciousness, are incomprehensible and inexpressible in words or concepts. Their well-earned prize will be most befitting, for the liberation of Mother Earth to which they have consecrated themselves—mind, body and spirit—will produce such a tremendous release of divine force in our solar system that the entire universe shall quiver in grateful response; all Creation, being inseparably connected, will be positively affected as every single life throughout the boundless Cosmos will, on some level, be gracefully and irreversibly touched.

> *"Behold the great key-keeper of the age has turned the key; the mighty gates fly wide and all who will may greet the King. Blessed are the pure in heart, for they shall see the King. Take heed! Be strong in mind; be pure in heart; be vigilant in helpfulness; the kingdom is at hand."*—Jesus.

Opposing Forces

AS GREATER LIGHT continues to illuminate the planetary consciousness, darkness is necessarily accentuated, for where there is light there must exist its corresponding shadow, or contrast, for in a dualistic universe one cannot exist and is meaningless without the other. More specifically, there has existed for millions of years a great protective barrier of spiritual force around our planet that was instigated and has been dutifully maintained by the Earth's own planetary Hierarchy. This ethereal bulwark regulates the incoming flow of various energies, forces and souls to Earth, while it also functions as a shield from cosmic evil. Without such a measure humanity would have experienced much greater oppression and hardship than that which it has known heretofore. In this time leading up to the birth of the New World, certain *doorways* are being opened in the barrier in order to allow for a larger influx of benign entities into our Earthly spheres where their aid may be rendered. However, these doorways are presently also being used for access by entities who are rather less than friendly, even though such wayward souls have the karmic right to be here on Earth.

The Divine Plan for planet Earth has to date been greatly retarded by the opposing forces. Today, however, the deadline for an intermediate consummation of that Plan is nigh, hence the present intensified activity of the dark forces everywhere upon the planet. In being aware of the expanding light upon the horizon of the old world, the forces of darkness are today redoubling their efforts against all that is good and righteous by trying all kinds of new, devious and desperate attempts to further delay the unfolding Divine Plan, and to take for themselves as much of the new light coming to the planet as they are able to snatch away from humanity. Servers are high-priority targets for the dark forces, of course, due to the inherent threat that they pose to the dominion of evil upon Earth, and consequently Servers will find that they generally receive attention from the *brothers of shadow* before that of Divinity. Characteristically, those of the dark side are most unscrupulous and merciless in their actions; they are ever keen to utilize absolutely any method that may further their insidious plot to inflict the greatest damage possible upon those virtuous souls who are regarded by these short-sighted antagonists as adversaries.

Individuals with any trace of selfishness, e.g., fear, pride, etc., and even those bearing genuine goodwill but possessing weak, indecisive or rigid and thus impressionable minds, are the easiest and, therefore, favorite victims of the opposing forces, and certain awakening Servers who have yet to reconsecrate their lives in service to the Divine Plan are today being successfully victimized from the inner planes in order to minimize their chances of responding positively to their wake-up calls. As a result, these unsuspecting Servers may suffer a variety of emotional, psychological and even physical afflictions, ranging from headaches and unnatural fatigue to advanced occult possession. As the planetary deadline approaches and as all conditions upon Earth—both good and evil, Truth and falsehood—intensify, Servers who in their forgetfulness may have become severely impaired as personalities will be presented with one of two critical choices: they must either search for and find a genuinely serviceful group, the common focus to which they should selflessly dedicate their lives (thus effecting their own healing), or they may choose to remain in the sombre gloom of selfhood and uncertainty whereby they will eventually be withdrawn from the physical plane having failed their assignment. It should be understood well by all Servers who have yet to reunite with other kindred souls for the purposes of furthering the One Divine Work upon Earth, that true, spiritual group communion creates an impregnable protective energy field, effectively warding off all evil so that higher spiritual forces may successfully enter the physical plane. Such a radiatory field will be an indispensable asset to any group during the approaching and inevitable onslaught of malevolent and blindly-destructive powers.

✳ ✳ ✳

The opposing forces are certainly not estranged from the profitable advice contained in the proverb: *"a stitch in time saves nine."* For ages the brothers of shadow have regarded the underlying designs and intentions of the Divine Plan for Earth, paying particular attention to this current and concluding phase of a major cycle, and consequently they have been long-preparing for that which has been termed *Armageddon*[*] in the Bible.

These materialistic powers, which are ever pitted against spiritual progress, always tread the path of least resistance, and so they begin their maligned attack upon certain personalities at the very earliest opportunity: when the foetus is still building its new physical body in the womb. It has been scientifically proven that an unborn child experiences to a significant degree whatever the mother experiences, and thus negative influences aimed at specific individuals (particularly Servers) begin before birth via the parents. Such wilful interference generally continues throughout child-

---

[*]   Specifically, the word 'Armageddon' means *a final and conclusive battle between the forces of good and evil*; an entirely befitting description indeed for our times, and a struggle which more and more aware and sensitive individuals are today recognizing is already underway.

hood, and many Servers may recall particular traumatic incidents that occurred very early in their lives which, upon due reflection, they may discern are responsible for certain personal dispositions or impairments that still presently exist.

Surreptitiously then, a seed of fear may be planted within a Server's personality vehicle during childhood, and this often occurs most profoundly at about the age of six or seven years old when the child's emotional constitution begins to become integrated within the individual and so is able to be permanently infected. The basic intention of evil after it has struck its first blow is for the growth of its seed to be promoted within the impressionable child by its surrounding environment which, of course, includes family, friends and acquaintances, the negative influence of whom is often further assured by perpetual incitement by those residing within hidden quarters who strive, consciously or unconsciously, under the banner of the antichrist.* Emotional or psychological poisoning in the early

---

* The antichrist is not a single person or being; it is not the 'Devil' or 'Satan,' neither of whom actually exist, although a great number of entities continue to derive satisfaction from impersonating the mythical Lord of Darkness. The term 'antichrist' refers to all evil intelligence as it is expressed in the universe in direct opposition to the plans of the Cosmic Christ— *The Lord of the World*—who is not the personality called Jesus, but an exalted field of divine Consciousness—a Great Being of Love and Wisdom—one tiny ray from whom shone through the lower vehicles of Jesus, as it did through those of the *Avatar*, Krishna of India, before him, as well as many other great Servers throughout human history, thereby bestowing upon these individuals the spiritual title of *world-saviour*. The word 'Christ' is derived from the Greek 'Kristos' meaning *The Anointed One*. Those who work under the banner of the antichrist include a whole host of sentient beings, some of whom are very advanced in terms of their occult knowledge, their power to control certain lesser spirits, and their ability to wield various natural forces; others may be quite unaware of how they are secretly used by the brothers of shadow, but all of them have one thing in common: selfishness, while those of a more treacherous nature harbour an insatiable lust for power, personal aggrandizement and dominion over others. It is, in fact, their innate selfishness that prevents any real and permanent alliance among them, and this is why the forces of darkness are always ultimately defeated by the greater united power of those who serve the Divine Plan, and who constitute, therefore, the divine Forces of Righteousness.

stages of a child's development may so easily create serious character disorders that, in turn, provide a doorway through which agents of evil may further infect the Server by negative occult impression. In so fortifying the personality weaknesses of the imitation ego, an attempt is made to render Servers incapable of fulfilling their spiritual duty later in life.

A common pattern experienced by Servers is that of years of unreasonable persecution and abuse by others who may sometimes even appear to have a perfectly irrational personal hatred for them due to the provocation of unseen entities who are themselves at the mercy and command of masters of evil. Such violations over extended periods do little to nurture a positive and loving attitude in many Servers, and today a large number of them demonstrate various levels of psycho-emotional infirmity, which is, of course, exactly what was intended by the opposing forces. Yet it should not be forgotten that, prior to the voluntary adoption of the veil of forgetfulness in physical embodiment, the likely incidence of such negative interference was fully apprehended and accepted by each Server as being an intrinsic factor of their sacrificial mission. All Servers understood well how evil minds seek to incite fear, doubt, anger and the like in their victims, thus rendering them easy to control; yet they also knew how all damage to the lower vehicles of consciousness could be effectively healed. Today, it is time for Servers to recollect that knowledge in order that they may be better prepared to help a world in need.

However, as is so prevalently the case amongst humanity today, Servers may also subconsciously block painful experiences from their awareness in order to avoid dealing with distressful memories. Yet these memories must be recalled for resolution as part of the process of remembrance in order that understanding, acceptance and forgiveness may effect complete release and consequent healing. Servers who embark upon the path of purification and healing will achieve greater ability to help others in *their* healing process, and the unprecedented grace available to all humanity at this time, delivered courtesy of the intensifying waves of new Aquarian energy, assures that healing and complete restoration may, for each and every individual, be swiftly realized; unselfish service is the key.

As was mentioned earlier, at this climactic time upon Earth the planet is a very busy focal point of galactic attention. Both benign entities and those who are oriented toward evil are today contacting their representatives upon Earth for correspondingly divine or selfish ends. Many Servers are discovering that they are able to be mediums (or 'channels' as they are now more usually termed) for the receipt of communications from various sources. Such individuals should remain well aware that even if they are genuinely oriented toward service to others, nevertheless in less spiritually-inspired moments they may still receive messages and interference in the form of lies or, at best, distortions of the Truth from entities who are far from enlightened.

Channelling, as it is widely practised today, is a low-grade psychic expression. It is one of the least demanding 'spiritual paths'; it is easy and therefore of negligible influence upon evolutionary progress and does not in the least assist Servers with their most vital duty upon Earth, which is to invoke and transmit divine energy in the world. In stark contrast, divine contact has ever been the prime goal of the serious spiritual aspirant, and this rule is especially pertinent to awakening Servers. Being the most direct communication with the Spirit for humanity, divine contact grants one the privilege of receiving pure insight, flawless intuition and dependable wisdom, obviating the need to communicate with other beings for information. Conversely, channelling can be very detrimental to the individual upon the path of holy service for numerous reasons, and, once divine contact has been attained, becomes completely superfluous.*

All forms of mediumship constitute a distraction to real spiritual attainment, and for Servers today channelling is fraught with danger. Moreover, the *trance* condition that many lesser mediums effortlessly adopt, is a most undesirable state, especially in these times. It separates the medium from his own soul and relegates him to the realms of unwholesome and material forces that abound upon the astral plane—*the realm of illusion*. It is imperative that mental activity and purity of heart be rapidly enhanced so that intelligent and conscious channelling may be practised safely if at all, otherwise true spiritual mediumship will remain a rare occurrence during the birth of the New World. The naïveté and excited grasping of the majority of those who are interested in channelling today, together with the ingenuousness, pride and selfishness of so many mediums, exposes groups to very definite dangers as they continue to let loose upon the world forces and entities of an

---

* Due recognition is given to the fact that some accurate and very useful information is presently being received through bona fide mediums. However, it should not be overlooked that this is only *information*. Channelling, in and of itself, does not constitute a path of spiritual development.

unholy nature.

It cannot be too strongly emphasized that all manner of guileful spirits upon the inner side of life are today proceeding to seek out and to contact sensitives in physical incarnation who evidence reasonable potential to become instruments for the execution of their ungracious plans, just as benevolent forces in service to the Divine Plan are searching for selfless and devoted hearts to help with the real divine Work upon Earth. As the lower psychic faculties of Servers—stimulated by the new energies—begin to expand, evil intelligences may eagerly rush in where angels will not tread. Wherever there exists even just a trace of selfishness in the consciousness of a medium, he or she becomes automatically prone to be deceived, used, victimized and even permanently possessed. Conditions are so ripe upon this eve of the New Day and humanity's gullibility and desire so pronounced and prevalent that such unfortunate occult usurpations are being facilitated by a *negative synergy* actualized by unprepared groups of perhaps well-meaning people. This is resulting in group possessions and it is to be observed today that certain mediums, together with some of their loyal followers, are headed straight for the lunatic asylum!

However, loving assistance is always at hand and ready to confer complete protection, even upon the dark planet. Selfless invocative appeal (which a humble and serviceful attitude engenders) will always attract divine attention and aid wherever necessary, and psychic attack of a superficial nature is generally the worst that negative entities may inflict upon those who are earnestly and wholeheartedly dedicated to helping others spiritually. The success of any assault made by the dark forces is directly proportional to the degree of self-regard that the intended victim may express. Selfish thoughts and emotions only serve to lower one's vibratory rate of consciousness, consequently rendering a person easy prey to the more gross frequencies of energy of the various planes that are utilized by entities with malefic intent in all their offensives.

※ ※ ※

It is evident that there has been an extreme patriarchal imbalance upon Earth for a very long time. The innate creative and intuitive qualities of the feminine spirit have been long-feared by distorted male perception, and as a result women have been repressed, dominated and persecuted throughout history. In order to bring equilibrium to a world that has known so much control by the male force, the majority of Server-souls upon Earth at this time have chosen to incarnate in female bodies.* As agents of change, these valiant envoys of the New Spirit bring to the planet a very high concentration of feminine power that will presently resolve the patriarchal problem upon Earth once and for all, restoring much needed balance and harmony that will benefit everyone in the New World, both women *and* men. During the time leading up to the Great Transition, however, and since male authority is still presently the controlling global power, female Servers will continue to experience something of the anguish of the collective persecution endured by so many women over the ages. Nonetheless, they are assured that their long-awaited time of liberation and victory is today at hand.

Female Servers often possess an inherent sympathetic attraction to mates who are in great need of love, healing and personal attention, yet who also harbour negative personality traits that may or may not include the syndrome of male dominance. There lies great potential danger within such attached compassion in relationships, even though the personal program is often designed to lead some women into direct experience of this kind. Blind anxiousness to be of service may result in very deleterious partnerships whereby the female Server is in danger of becoming completely overshadowed and *vampirized* (drained of life-force) by her partner due to debilitating chakra interplay and auric contamination as she earnestly attempts to help a man who is unable to receive her love. Evil influence operates effortlessly and efficiently through males who har-

---

* The process of seeding the New World Consciousness requires far fewer male Servers in incarnation than female. It may be recognized that this is a pervasive design of Nature; it is exemplified by multifarious species of life around the world, and operates under the Law of Reproduction. A vast number of different classes of animals, fish, birds and insects (as well as humanity itself) demonstrate that during one single sexual act, millions of spermatozoa are released for potential fertilization of the female ovum. The birth of the New World Consciousness is, of course, an esoteric phenomenon, but nevertheless follows the same natural pattern as that of many physical-plane life-forms. In other words, it takes just one male Server to produce a profusion of *life-sparks* bearing the potential to spiritually inseminate many female Servers, and to thus conceive the New World Consciousness.

bour tendencies of the lower self, and victimization is a very common outcome of the typically submissive disposition demonstrated by many female Servers in the world today, and may easily inflict much psycho-emotional damage. Lingering for too long within harmful relationships that are not progressive may be fatal to the Server's mission, and many women will find that they shall have to terminate their relationships, leaving their partners behind during the forthcoming transitions.

* * *

Today, as mankind is awakening in accord with the approaching Harvest Time and the greatest spiritual opportunity ever upon Earth, members of the opposing forces are, with remarkable alacrity, stepping forward to inaugurate themselves to the general public as spiritual leaders and healers. They are well-practised at skillfully masquerading their true intentions with a veil of inspiring melodramas and emotionally-appealing deceptions of all kinds. It is one of their favorite and most frequently employed ruses to pose as holy messengers, for they know well how to appeal to humanity's gullibility, desire and pride. They often impersonate the qualities and missions of true Servers of the Divine Plan, proudly announcing themselves as 'walk-ins,' angels, starseeds, etc., publishing exciting and authoritative books, giving lectures and workshops to large groups of people, and even effecting what might seem upon the surface to be truly humanitarian works. Many of those who are offering false teachings in the world today are all the more convincing to the unaware due to the fact that they themselves actually believe what they teach, and may therefore possess genuinely sincere motives. Yet while they forge ahead with the notion that they really are serving the Divine Plan, in their myopia and essentially selfish orientation and ignorance they are in fact little more than human marionettes for the brothers of shadow. Other contemporary teachers are quite conscious of their own ulterior motives, which are always aimed at engendering craving, attachment, blind obedience, subordination and so on, and these imposters delight in creating the lure of that which is attractive to the personal self as they deliberately attempt to block the influx of anything which is true and holy.

These devious antagonists of all that is real and good and true are especially keen to divert Servers from their path. They know well that awakening Servers are presently seeking to understand their new and unfolding consciousness, and so they are making great efforts to effectively distort the truth of the awakening process and to thus lead as many Servers astray as possible. This is accomplished by offering impressive yet false and often complex philosophical systems and substitutes for Truth that may appear to be helpful and authentic to many, but which are in fact designed to induce a passion, however subtle, for self-gratification, thus lowering the vibratory rate of consciousness and leading to disempowerment, blindness and dependency. These shrewd deceivers amongst us today seek to at least neutralize the Servers' mission, while their preference is to utterly crush and destroy anything that is in alignment with the Divine Plan for Earth. They are disseminating all kinds of very interesting information in their campaign to ensnare and distract as many individuals, groups and organizations as they are able from the most simple, unchanging and spiritually-sound message of love and service. They may also perform miraculous healings and demonstrate psychic powers in order to inspire faith in the masses, and to subsequently win the adulation and allegiance of the naïve.

What may be regarded as miraculous by some, however, is nothing but a metaphysical dynamic that is responsible for the harnessing of natural forces; faith acts as both a magnifier and a conductor, and makes this dynamic possible. Just as electricity—which is potentially present everywhere—becomes effective only in the presence of a conductor, so 'supernatural' power becomes effective only in the presence of faith, be it faith in a human teacher, in the divine intelligence immanent in Creation, faith in an ideal or even in one's own spiritual nature. History attests to the fact that blind faith may be easily and promptly cultivated amongst the credulous, desirous or needy. If a true divine experience has yet to be attained, the exuberant and hopeful self-seeker may easily confuse lower-astralism and psychic phenomena for spiritual revelation and holy wisdom. Furthermore, those cunning entities who are sworn enemies of truth and righteousness understand very well how selfishly-motivated faith may be exploited and used like a kind of vacuum that draws certain surrounding forces into itself, thus endowing the individual or group with which it is connected with various etheric and astral energies that are naught but imitations of those higher forces in which the faith has been invested.

It is a fact that in order to instigate and maintain their power and charisma, spiritual and religious leaders depend as much on the faith of their adherents as their adherents depend on the initial inspiration which they may receive from their leaders. Once this mutually profitable affair has begun, it can easily expand to allure and subsequently influence many other aspirants who may be attracted (or magnetically pulled in) to the psychically-charged atmosphere that is so common within such groups. The subsequent magnification of synergetic potency will be in direct proportion to the degree of emotional charge peculiar to the group, as well as the will and manipulative abilities of the leader(s). Therefore, it is not difficult to see how the combined forces evoked by those whose faith is directed toward a spiritual 'superior' make him a centre of power that goes far beyond that of his own personality, while simultaneously also providing a convenient conduit for the brothers of shadow to enter and influence our world. Selfish spirituality is *imitation spirituality*, and is today epidemic in the world, both within the New Age movement as well as in more traditional religious circles.

Religious intermediaries and spiritual leaders are still employed today due to humanity's ignorance of universal laws, and as long as such blindness persists in the world, black magicians, false spiritual teachers and bogus religions will continue to proliferate in response to mankind's desire. A rapidly growing number of false prophets and unscrupulous mystics are presently rising in power all around the world. Due to the pervasive ingenuousness and craving of humanity, these sorcerers are successfully wielding occult forces not for the common good, but for their own selfish ends, and they are consequently leading many people farther and farther away from divine Truth and genuine spiritual experience by offering a *cold light*, which can be remarkably convincing to those who do not look to their own heart for verification. These mock-Servers are bringing about the fulfilment of the New Testament prophecy that at the time of the end *"even the wise will be led astray"* and that there will be much distortion of the truth concerning the spread of the New World Consciousness.

It is of vital importance at this late stage of the current phase of the Divine Plan for Earth that Servers hearken to their conscience: the voice of Divinity within. They should pursue only their highest and most selfless aspirations, trusting and following the urging of their personal program which will guide them forward safely amidst all the contrived allurements and snares that have been set along the path especially for them, but which cannot fool the person who has attained true Knowledge and whose sights are set on helping the world. Amidst so much world delusion and spiritual inertia upon this, their culminating Earthly mission, Servers who are struggling to uncover and reveal the Truth in order to free others and themselves, will necessarily receive similar blows to those dealt to and endured by the martyrs of yesteryear. However, man grows strong by the buffetings of life, and the steel of the soul is tempered in the fire of Earthly experience. The Servers' challenging task demands that on occasion they stand apparently alone, yet to those who persevere to the end in faith and dedication to the One Great Cause—ever undaunted by the slanderous accusations and venom of the beast's desperate and dying throes—success is assured.

> "The storm of wrath comes on; you shall be maltreated by the scribes and Pharisees, the high priests and the doctors of the law. Without a cause you will be haled into the courts and cast into prison cells; you will be stoned; you will be beaten in the synagogues; will stand condemned before the rulers of this world, and governors and kings shall sentence you to death. But you will falter not, and you will testify for truth and righteousness. And when these times shall come let wisdom guide; do not resent. Resentment makes more strong the wrath of evil men. There is a little sense of justice and of mercy in the vilest men of Earth. By taking heed to what you do and say, and trusting in the guidance of the Holy Breath, you may inspire this sense to grow. You thus may make the wrath of men to praise the Lord." — Jesus.

The Great Risk

REWARDS FOR SERVICE successfully rendered by servers upon Earth are not insubstantial. Due to the fact that there exist a multitude of trials and challenges upon the planet, especially at this time, significant spiritual merit and progress will be known by those diligent Servers who fulfil their mission. At the same time, however, the descent into third-density reality entails great risk, particularly for those Servers who are well beyond the need for physical-plane lessons. Indeed, every single soul that becomes exposed to the great temptations and negative influences upon the dark planet is in danger of accruing new and undesirable karma. Planet Earth could be regarded as a kind of intensive training school that promotes rapid progress for all who choose to act wisely when opportunities are presented, and this is well and good for those Servers who respond positively and selflessly to their wake-up calls. However, the most dire and grievous danger with which Servers upon Earth are threatened is that of actual spiritual retrogression, and this is a very real peril acknowledged by all Servers prior to their voluntary incarnation.

Affected by the pervasive, negative influence of the opposing forces upon Earth today, many Servers are themselves fluctuating around or even receding from the minimum vibratory rate required for their successful harvest from third-density reality. This is mainly due to spiritual sloth and, therefore, self-protracted forgetfulness. Instead of proceeding forth in dedicated usefulness to humanity and thereby helping others to rise with them to greet the New Dawn, many Servers today remain quite oblivious of their own identity and duty to the world. In their inertia they are not only in danger of jeopardizing their personal mission and nullifying some of the positive cumulative effects of their own efforts made perhaps over many incarnations, but they are also accountable for failing their group soul. As if this were not unfortunate enough, the most devastating consequence of a Server's perpetual slumber is that they risk becoming displaced for an indefinite period, perhaps irretrievably, amidst the tarrying stream of souls who fail to meet the requirements for success at the Harvest Time. Servers who have accrued new karma in their forgetfulness are in danger of both failing to be harvested themselves and so of being compelled by karmic law to reincarnate again in the future upon a physical planet alongside those of humanity who similarly fail to graduate. Such is the eminent risk taken by all Servers who have descended from their home-density in order to assist humanity's transition at this time; a venture entailing the very great peril of becoming relegated for an unforeseeable number of incarnations to a lower level of existence than that from which they originated at the commencement of their voluntary mission. It is presently vital, therefore, that unawakened Servers accept the help offered to them by others from their own or kindred soul-groups who will be guided to assist in their reawakening at this most critical time.

The danger of becoming karmically entangled upon the physical plane constitutes the greatest challenge that all Servers must face, and, following their departure from Earth after the planetary deadline, fallen Servers confront untold delay upon life's everlasting road. Any consciously unloving thought, feeling or action creates unfavorable karmic repercussions. The critical need for Servers to understand the nature of the serious dangers to which they are constantly exposed during their mission, and the vital requirement for them to discern well the corresponding opportunities that these dangers present, cannot be over-emphasized. In order for success to be known, Servers must learn to see through the illusion of separation that is inherent within third-density experience, and to practise acceptance and love through all apparent dualities. Love is the greatest aid to remembrance for Servers, and all would do well to bear in mind always that only unconditional love is karma-free!

It is an immutable requirement of cosmic law that all karma must be balanced within the density in which it was accrued: "*As ye sow, so shall ye reap.*" Today, a great number of Servers are teetering on the edge of a great chasm between success and failure. Many, in their forgetfulness, have indeed attracted new and deleterious karma to themselves while upon Earth, either in their present incarnation or during previous lifetimes. *It is imperative that such individuals understand well that they are living in times of unprecedented grace, and that all of their past karma may be swiftly resolved as never before should they make the right decisions today.* The Aquarian energies are most conducive to the rapid release of past detrimental psychological and emotional patterns. However, should Servers fail to prepare themselves for the receipt of this grace, should they continue to remain in self-regard or to react in ignorance to symptoms of purification, and consequently should they fail to balance every last karmic debt before Judgement Day, then it is guaranteed that they will know an incompatibility with the group-soul of which they were once a part as it prepares to rise into the next level of evolutionary experience which it may have collectively merited.

During the inevitable evolutionary process whereby the group-soul makes claim to its grand investment made long ago, those tainted parts of itself (i.e., Servers who have become karmically contaminated) will necessarily be rejected from graduating along with the greater whole. Due to the unresolved karmic residue that will have become an integral part of their consciousness, these Servers will separate from their group-soul and, by law, they will have to reincarnate in lower vibratory spheres in order to balance their newly-acquired karma.

Such a downgrading certainly imposes a considerable, though incalculable, delay to the onward journey of those concerned; yet while such delay is unquestionably serious and unfortunate, nevertheless the universal Law of Recompense knows no biased leniency and so can show no special sympathy for those who do not *make the grade*. Such blighted Server-souls who are necessarily expelled from the ongoing life-stream of their group are clearly in need of more experience within the lower worlds, and that experience they will be given, even though it may mean innumerably additional lifetimes within these grosser spheres, many of which will be dreary and may include much suffering.

Such, then, is the very worst possible outcome of a Server's voluntary mission; that they may become lost alongside other straggling souls who similarly cannot enter the New World for an indefinite period. However, let it now be reiterated to every single Server in every part of the world that opportunity is being given today by the unparalleled grace of the times. May each and every Server recognize the call to service and, in subsequently utilizing their own free will wisely and selflessly, may they become a contributing asset to the now imminent *Victory of Ages*, and may they thus secure their own spiritual graduation at the Harvest Time.

New Teachings and a New Way

ALL THAT IS NEW—philosophy, religion, science, spirituality, etc.—is today revealing itself in conspicuous contrast to the old and outworn standards as a major division develops on a grand scale. Unremittingly the split between the two yawns steadily wider and begins to evidence itself now prominently in the physical world. Such a division is apparent to those who are aware and who therefore recognize the current indications of what must ultimately transpire.

As Earth-frequencies rise, and as new, subtle yet potent forces pour into the invisible planes corresponding to our physical planet, a new order of life is emerging; a new awareness and a greater appreciation of the interconnectivity of all Creation is growing within the minds of humanity. Outmoded ways of the past are rapidly proving themselves unworthy of the new realities and thus are nullifying themselves through a process of atrophy that will eventuate in their complete and permanent eradication from planet Earth. The old cannot withstand the new, for such is the Divine Plan for our world. A brand new life-paradigm is dawning within the planetary consciousness today, and everyone who recognizes and lives by the new truths will learn much from the demise of the old.

Those who are gravitating toward the emerging new world paradigm are presently seeking to find out more, and this search for new and greater understanding is something that absolutely everyone would undertake if they were not so immersed in the great plethora of worldly distractions. This is so because the impetus to seek and thus to grow is an essential quality of the divine Spirit, and so is also inherent within every soul. To become aware of the grand possibilities of spiritual seeking is to be onto something; to fail to be onto something is to live an empty life. It may be clearly recognized, therefore, that an open and inquisitive attitude is ever necessary if rigidity and stagnation are to be avoided and spiritual progress assured. Such is the inborn and natural instinct of a child, without which it would never grow emotionally, mentally or spiritually. Similarly, in adulthood, the seeking of greater meaning in life is essential to spiritual advancement. Refraining from seeking any higher purpose other than mere survival, pleasure and procreation is to experience spiritual death. Seeking, therefore, is synonymous with progress, and ultimately will reveal life's purpose. Like humanity, Servers will also remain incarcerated within the shadows of ignorance if they do not uncompromisingly seek the Truth. The very act of seeking sets forces in motion that greet the seeker in order to reveal certain *secrets* which that individual may be ready to behold; life responds as if to an invitation. By self-initiated efforts to move forward into grander regions of spiritual reality, the intuitive faculty is automatically stimulated and the seeker's vibratory rate of consciousness is raised as awareness expands. Regardless of their cultural background, such is the fundamental understanding of all true prophets, seers and saints who naturally and spontaneously invoke Revelation by their humble inquiry into Existence, and the seed of every true religion or spiritual teaching has been produced in this way.

Now, the Great Jewel of Truth has many facets, all of which reflect the One Light of the Universal Mind. Spanning the vast expanses of time and shining upon all countries of the world through the hearts and souls of pioneers belonging to multifarious races of men, these reflections of the One Truth have been perceived in a multitude of different ways depending upon a variety of factors. These factors include social perspective, ethnic influence, the period in world history (and therefore the level of human development) or even the personal disposition of a single individual who may have been initially responsible for motivating the masses toward a new and brighter awareness. Consequently, and as long as the evolutionary current proceeds, new religions, cosmologies and spiritual philosophies will always arise, each one offering a distinctive presentation of the unchanging Ageless Wisdom: the Eternal Truth.

Humanity, however, in its habitual practise of tampering with those things that are already perfect just as they are, has repeatedly misinterpreted and consequently contaminated all of the true religious dispensations given out by various individuals or groups throughout history. This has been perpetrated, sometimes over centuries, by adding to, taking from, diluting, exaggerating or otherwise modifying the simple verities expounded within certain authenticated and established religious works. Such is an enduring fact, even though millions today might swear that their chosen doctrine or 'gospel' is pure and intact. It is significant also that these same adherents may often be just as quick to point out the flaws and falsities in other religions that are different from their own and so perhaps little understood by them. Such a psychology is, of course, responsible for provoking all religious tensions, segregations, wars and persecutions. Religion is not to blame, mankind's short-sighted interpretation of religious doctrine is. Consequently, there is once again today an urgent need for fresh, true and undistorted spiritual teachings; teachings that will restore the sacred Essence of past religious dogma and so help to unite the various presentations of the One Universal Truth that lies at the foundation of all true religious dispensations, past, present and future.

> *"Let us not fear to reject from our religion all that is useless, material, tangible as well as all that is vague and indefinite; the more we purify its spiritual kernel, the more we shall understand the true Law of Life."* — Tolstoy.

Tseng Tse expresses a similar sentiment: *"One should not think that a religion is true because it is old. On the contrary the more mankind lives, the more the true Law of Life becomes clear to him. To suppose that in our epoch one must continue to believe what our grandfathers and ancestors believed is to think that an adult can continue to wear the garments of children."*

Times change, and so does consciousness. It is a most worthwhile and indeed necessary measure today to prepare our *vessels* so that they may be worthy to contain the *new wine* that is being poured most liberally upon everyone alike from the *heavens*. A full or closed vessel cannot receive any new wine, and the children of the New World therefore remain open and stand ready for the instant recognition of that which is new and true. They are eager for the immediate grasp of the truth of the times and they are in preparation for the treading of the New Way in the unfoldment of the pioneering human consciousness, and for the revelation—steadily and constantly presented by the emerging life—of the new and superseding ideas. These ideas possess a dynamic expulsive power and are, therefore, the natural adversary of the old and obsolete, as all dedicated Servers will testify, but they do meet human needs more than adequately in the new cycle.

In the words of Thoreau: *"How astonishing is this that of all the supreme revelations of truth, the world admits and tolerates only the more ancient, those which answer least to the needs of our epoch, while it holds each direct revelation, each original thought for null, and sometimes hates them."*

The attitude of all awakening individuals today is set for the prompt relinquishing of all that is futile, unnecessary and inadequate to the need of the hour, and for the reception of that Power from on-high which necessarily breaks and destroys everything that has become crystallized, that has served its purpose fully, and which is consequently redundant. Awakened Servers are therefore ready to work as dedicated servants of the Divine Plan in accord with all that is new and relevant, reaching out compassionately in service to humanity by holding up the true vision of the Aquarian age for all to see, and by thus living earnestly in accord with their purpose on Earth.

Resulting from the beneficent influence of the Aquarian energies upon mankind's consciousness, much new inspiration is today being experienced by those individuals who have been actively seeking the Truth as it applies to the present level of world development. As has already been intimated, Truth reveals itself to the sincerely-seeking mind and heart and, like the prophets of yore, new and creative insights are being received at this time all over the world by those who have learned (or recalled) how to successfully harmonize their lives in accord with universal law, and particularly with the new and adjusted laws of the Aquarian age for Earth. Such discoveries are today evoking positive action in the lives of these harbingers of that which is new and better for the planet as they embrace the responsibility of meeting the requirements of the present, and of serving humanity by sharing the truth that has been revealed to them.

The spiritual needs of our times are today being widely broadcast by such heralds as they proceed to honour their duty to mankind. While conscientiously acting as agents of the New Spirit, these servants of the race are helping to birth the New Way of conscious spiritual progress upon Earth. This New Way incorporates inspired and practical methodologies that duly accommodate the New World Consciousness, the adjusted laws of the new era, and all the various modern conditions that will continue to manifest in the Aquarian age.

As the expanding awareness of humanity is beginning to regard life in the light of spiritual values, new teachings have commenced their foreordained precipitation around the planet, and certain elements of these new teachings are now being offered to mankind everywhere in the world by awakening Servers. These seeds of the New Way will eventually grow into a verdant garden bearing many fruits, one of which shall be the forthcoming new religion* that will offer tomorrow's humanity a fresh and truer understanding of the Divine Plan, together with a living insight into the great lives and minds of those who implement it upon Earth, and who are the engineers of mankind's future.

The best of the virtues and advantages of past religious dispensations will be brought forward into the New World and updated, taking due consideration of the new realities. The new religion will be a world religion. With the spread of unity consciousness as well as the rise of greater intelligence and awareness generally upon the planet, no longer will mankind be so disposed to segregate itself by multifarious and complex presentations of the One Universal Truth, as has been the case in the past and to great disadvantage worldwide. Free of dogma and distinguished not by doctrines, the New World religion will not be exemplified by theological psychologies or through organized sectarian groups and churches, but by an earnestly loving inner attitude and a natural orientation toward the truly spiritual life.

The New Way will be scientifically-based, i.e., it will elicit greater practical insight into the Ageless Wisdom and will represent esoteric principles that will be proven by application and subsequent experience. When the Truth is seen together, the hearts of humanity become united. As inspired religious ceremonies and prayers take place at the same hour with common understanding and with identical spiritual intent all around the globe, the powerful collective invocation of the united family of humanity will penetrate far deeper into the hidden worlds and more than ever before will evoke a correspondingly profound response from divine spheres. In demanding attention and succor from the higher planes, such forceful and vertical appeal will assist in the reinstatement and preservation of *"Heaven on*

---

* The word 'religion' is derived from the Latin *'religare'* and means to *re-link* or *reunite*. True religion offers a dependable spiritual system for alignment and unification with the Divine. It lucidly and unequivocally presents the truth of universal law and, unlike most existing religious dispensations, is not formulated or utilized to control people. Therefore, the new religion should not be compared to those extant today which are actually but shades of their pure and original form.

Earth," and this New Way will emerge fully when humanity is ready to really live its teachings.

The process of preparation for the healing, upliftment and liberation of mankind in the New World must necessarily incorporate new and practical guidance that will inspire an uncompromising inner search for true understanding. Blind faith, deferential belief and unthinking conformity will be mercifully absent from the New World Consciousness, and the intelligible comprehensiveness and conciseness of the New World religion will help to encourage and maintain such a lucid awareness during the Aquarian cycle. When humanity begins to appreciate and, therefore, live by the immutable laws of Life due to its own inspired personal enquiry into Reality, an unshakable trust in that Life will develop, and divine contact will ultimately result from the consequent intelligent surrender to and cooperation with divine Order. Such an alignment with universal law begets identification with the Greater Self in all, and thus gives rise to the experience of unconditional love, that most sublime expression of the divine Spirit which ever seeks to give of itself for the benefit of others. Since they will live for the world, individuals who attune to the New Way of spiritual progress in the Aquarian era will be naturally motivated from within to help their fellows, and so it is that the global community on Earth will be born.

The New World Consciousness will become fully established upon Earth soon after the critical mass has been assembled and when mankind is therefore ready to welcome and contribute toward positive change. The pioneering work of Servers will then swiftly increase and spread, this being reflected in an expansion of their breed and in the consequent diffusion throughout the world of goodwill, charity, altruism and worldwide selfless collaboration. The joint efforts of Servers will contribute significantly toward the clear discernment, comprehension, and active resolution of all injustice upon the planet, and will culminate in the permanent transmutation of evil and in the engendering of wholesome and symbiotic human relationships. Such a conscious alignment with the designs of the universe together with the intelligent application in life of its laws, will produce a conducive global spiritual climate that will facilitate the long-awaited manifestation of Divinity upon Earth.

Speaking of the "New Church" of the Aquarian age, the following prophetic vision for our time was left by the Cathars, the last known of whom were burned alive by the Inquisition of the Roman Catholic Church at Montsegur, Languedoc, France in 1244 AD:

It has no fabric, only understanding.

It has no membership, save those who know they belong.

It has no rivals, because it is non-competitive.

It has no ambition, it seeks only to serve.

It knows no boundaries, for nationalisms are unloving.

It is not of itself, because it seeks to enrich all groups and religions.

It has no secret, no arcanum, no initiation save that of true understanding of the power of love and that, if we want it to be so, the world will change, but only if we change ourselves first.

It acknowledges all great teachers of all ages who have shown the truth of love.

Its participants will practise the truth of love in all their being.

It seeks not to teach but to be, and in being, to enrich.

It recognizes the whole planet as a Being of which we are all a part.

It recognizes that the time has come for the supreme transmutation, the ultimate alchemical act of conscious change of the world-ego into a voluntary return to the Whole.

It does not proclaim itself with a loud voice, but in the subtle realms of loving.

It salutes all those in the past who have blazed the path and have paid the price.

Its members shall know each other by their deeds and being, and by their eyes, and by no other outward sign save the fraternal embrace.

Its members will dedicate their lives to the silent loving of their neighbor and environment and the planet, while carrying out their task, however exalted or humble.

It recognizes the supremacy of the Great Idea which may only be accomplished if the human race practises love.

It has no reward to offer either here or in the hereafter save that of the ineffable joy of being and loving.

Its members shall seek to advance the cause of understanding, doing good by stealth, and teaching only by example.

Its members shall heal their neighbors, their community and

our planet.
Its members shall know no fear and feel no shame, and their knowledge shall prevail over all odds.
All those who belong, belong to the church of love.

The True Path

IT IS ANTICIPATED that the disclosures within this book may assist Servers in recognizing themselves by their life patterns. In thus comprehending the reasons for their past experiences, struggles and unusual perceptions they may see the wisdom in commencing the great adventure of seeking further. Servers who are today witnessing a growing sense that there is something very worthwhile to be discovered by them and who follow that inner impulse forward into life's greatest Mystery, will find that they are most certainly not alone in their presentiments. Since the act of seeking Truth automatically hones the sixth sense and clarifies one's vision, Servers are likely to begin recognizing members of their own spiritual family shortly after they have made a firm commitment to embark upon the all-important quest for understanding; a most splendid and necessary pilgrimage that a great many Servers have already begun today or are right now preparing for.

When the Servers' uncompromising decision to move forward spiritually has been registered within the hidden worlds, they will be given assistance, not only by their own group-soul but also by other divine Agents who are close to the planet at this time and who are ever seeking to help. The Law of Synchronicity will begin to manifest once Servers commence the seeking process in earnest, and they will come to recognize that they are unequivocally guided and protected upon their path. This is assured because the sincere thirst for Knowledge and spiritual realization will have initiated a powerful and dependable invocation upon the higher planes which, by law, cannot be ignored by those who watch and wait.

However, if Servers truly yearn to live in harmony with divine law, and if they are to attain the greater heights of spiritual success, then they must clearly understand that their search cannot be made for their own sake. In order to know real spiritual fulfilment, one's own self must be forgotten, for in self-forgetfulness liberation is experienced: liberation from the separative ego, which is the source of all pain and sorrow. Now, if the self has been forgotten altogether, then one cannot be thinking about when or how that self should be set free, what kind of happiness it will have or what type of ascended Master it will become! Indeed, true and complete happiness must include the happiness of those around us and ultimately also that of each and every living thing with which we are inseparably connected. It is an immutable certainty that while there most certainly *is* freedom from the constricting laws of the lower self, there is no freedom from the divine Law of Relationship and from constant interplay between person and person, soul and soul, life and life. The greatest joy to be found in relationship with others is in helping them; real, spiritual happiness—or joy—may be found only in helpfulness, and all of life's many and diverse roads eventually converge upon the one Path of Service. The reasons for this will be made clear by the following elucidations.

There is an old dictum that warns: *"Never trust anyone who proclaims that they have found the only way that leads to God."* When considering the multifarious techniques of spiritual discipline that have been prescribed and successfully practised throughout history, the foregoing statement may appear to be quite correct. However, a deeper investigation by an informed mind that is able to elevate its thinking to a higher turn of the evolutionary spiral will reveal that its veracity only applies up to a certain point of spiritual attainment.

It has been repeatedly averred by all the religious teachings and enunciations of the great spiritual luminaries throughout mankind's history that individuality is really one with the Whole; it has been clearly pointed out that the belief in the illusion of an isolated self and the consequent indulging thereof is the cause of all separation and therefore suffering. Furthermore, should we pause to reflect upon the obvious fact that an infinitely larger portion of the Cosmos exists apart from the little self, then we are likely to appreciate the relative insignificance of that self as well as the enormously greater substance, magnitude and import with regard to all that is not of the personal self. With this in mind, the seemingly separate individual might recognize the wisdom in never having any interests that are opposed to the universal laws that guide and govern all of Creation. Of course, the selfishness of egotism is diametrically opposed to one such law: the sacred Law of Love, and so, just like one's own shadow, trouble will necessarily follow the transgressor of that law. Yet the plain truth is that in helping others lies our own greatest good, and spiritual aspirants are most truly progressing when they assist the progress of others. Such is the way of Love, that glorious cosmic principle under which the creation of each and every one of the innumerable worlds throughout Infinity is made possible, and as the divine force of Love itself silently permeates them all. The very quintessence of the universe, then, is Love, and it is Love, therefore, that must be embodied and expressed by each individual life at some stage during the course of its growth before the gateway leading to the True Path of Return may be traversed. *"He who counts his life of so much worth that he would give it not in willing sacrifice to save his brother man, is worthy not to enter into Life."* —Jesus.

Now, Love has an inseparable relationship with Truth, for Truth seen becomes Love expressed. The spiritual heart can never be truly and permanently satisfied until the experience of Love and Truth is shared perpetually with other manifestations of the One, and it may be recognized, therefore, that the way of loving service is the True Path of Holiness (wholeness) for which all other spiritual disciplines are but preparatory. This can be easily verified by due recognition of the historically recurring fact that all the greatest spiritual masters, saints and true teachers of the Way have trodden the most noble path of selfless service. For such enlightened ones it cannot be otherwise and, in time, it will be so for all humanity similarly, as each individual recognizes the Truth and so chooses to walk that same Road that has been graced by the hallowed feet of those who went forth before them to claim their own spiritual freedom.

* * *

As the Heart of Cosmic Being progressively unfolds itself through each soul in accordance with the universal and irresistible divine decree of spiritual evolution; as mankind necessarily ascends to greater heights of virtue and holiness; and as consciousness is inevitably elevated and sanctified throughout numerous incarnations of learning, each personality must necessarily become more divine, as a greater realization of the sacred essence of life is attained. This innermost essence—or Spirit—is the true nature of everything seen, sensed and yet to be discovered, and its most sublime expression is Love, which ever seeks to express itself in service.

Eternally, Love seeks to flow through all things, to touch other parts of itself, to kiss and to merge in sacred reunion. As the nature of mankind is spiritual, the Way of Love must eventually be found by each and every person, and it is only upon this path that the chalice of the heart becomes so full and overflowing with the ambrosial nectar of divine Love that it simply cannot be contained and there is always more than enough to be joyfully shared with everyone. Love is a most natural expression, and its passionate and enrapturing song is ever-waiting to spring from any open heart upon the path of selfless service.

A taste of even the tiniest droplet of pure Love forever impresses its divine nature within the heart, and when we begin to penetrate into the reality of the One Great Principle that pervades, loves and serves throughout the infinite universe, we shall be naturally disposed to attune ourselves with that magnificent law, and thus, in Love, we shall gladly embark upon the way of spiritual service. In fact, as our awareness is illumined by the light of Truth, we shall find that the sanest choice in life has been made automatically for us simply by our reverential surrender to the omnipresent, loving Will of Creation. A gently hushed and transcendental voice deep within ourselves will then whisper its sacred and profound yet simple secret to our waking consciousness, and we shall remember the wonderful Truth. At this blessed hour we will realize with the utmost felicity that we have at last struggled away from the mass of seekers of the Path and onto the Path itself. The battle that we have blindly waged against the loving current of evolution in our service to ourselves will finally come to an end as the real spiritual adventure that embraces the ever-expanding delight of renouncing the lower self for the True Self—the divine Spirit—will then begin, in service to the world.

Since everything in the universe is interconnected, such a personal realization becomes an immeasurable blessing to all life, and particularly to those forms with which the awakened individual comes into contact, yet the greatest spiritual benefit is bestowed upon the one who has become enlightened by the simple Truth. Their unprecedented good fortune includes the liberating revelation that instead of identifying themselves as a separate and struggling individual, alone in a competitive and hostile world, and instead of hopelessly striving for self against the ever-forward-flowing stream of life, they may now, with lucid recognition, consciously cooperate with Divinity as an integral part of its purposeful evolutionary intelligence, like a healthy cell in a great organism. This they may now do without hesitation because they have penetrated the veil of forgetfulness and remembered their own true, loving and compassionate nature by contacting the Spirit within. In such precious recollection, the exquisite perfection of Creation is revealed to them and a supreme and undying trust and confidence is born from an inner *knowing* which transcends the most pure and ardent religious faith. Before tear-filled eyes of spiritual elation and with unsurpassed gratitude, the blessedness of Existence then proceeds to unfold itself to the humbled beholder. In the subsequent attainment of a new and habitually reverent attitude toward all things, one's every thought, feeling, word and action become sacred as one's whole life is naturally consecrated to the Divine. Consequently, and at each moment, one is elevated by the Law of Recompense and, with the greatest joy, draws progressively nearer to complete remembrance and spiritual fulfilment.

At this stage it becomes apparent to the illumined mind that every deed that is performed with a pure and unselfish motive always yields favorable results for everyone concerned as it creates positive causes that subsequently reverberate forth along the corridor of time and on into a brighter future. Such is the enlightened understanding of a saint, yet that which is regarded as 'enlightenment' by many is recognized by those who see and know as just the beginning of an eternal and sacred journey. Enlightenment is not an end-product or result, but a continuing process of cumulative remembrance within the supernal light of spiritual reality, and such is the divine heritage of every sincere servant of Life. Enlightenment is a never-ending and joyful process of spiritual unfoldment, discovered only through the giving of Love to others; a Love that resides within the heart of every single soul in the world and can never be found by any outward grasping. Indeed, once something of the unbound unity and limitless nature of Creation has been understood, the notion of seeking to attain Truth, enlightenment or spiritual power for oneself alone is recognized as being wholly absurd. To the contrary, upon the dawning of true understanding, we shall gladly accept the one supreme honour, become most happily acquiescent in humbly taking our rightful place amidst the shining ranks of the Hierarchies of Servers throughout the multifarious spheres of the universe, and begin serving as we are able by starting from right where we are, as all the Great Ones have done before us.

* * *

Now, many aspirants in the world today believe that great spiritual benefit may be gained by practising certain meditative techniques and the like. While this may be quite true for those who are able to discipline themselves over a long period of time, these same adherents often overlook the fact that the most accomplished meditators have always emerged from their solitude in order to extend their meditation in *service* to the world. Theirs may be said to be the most supreme meditation of all, for it reflects the One

Great Eternal Meditation which endures within the Universal Mind itself, and has done ever since the blueprints for the Cosmos were conceived, i.e., even before its creation: a very long time indeed. Thus, the meditation of service appears to have been quite adequately tried, tested, successfully demonstrated and so verified as being a most pre-eminent practise, and this certification has been made by a rather higher Authority than any teacher upon Earth!

When one embarks upon the True Path of spiritual service and converges all one's energies upon it, progress is ensured without a single thought for self, and with remarkable ease when compared to one's previous struggle and limitation in the world of the separated ego. Indeed, one's own spiritual advancement becomes enormously accelerated due to such self-forgetfulness. When a person's free will is applied in accord with the divine Will, the rewards for all efforts made are multiplied exponentially because they are rendered in perfect alignment with universal law. Therefore the advancement of the individual will not be by arithmetical progression, i.e., 2, 4, 6, 8, etc., nor even by geometrical progression, i.e., in the ratio 2, 4, 8, 16, etc., but by powers in the order of the ratio 2, 4, 16, 256, 65536, etc.! Such is the grace bestowed upon all servants of the Divine Plan as they proceed upon their ministry of joy. This is due only to the fact that they have offered themselves up as humble instruments for active service, thereby setting up favorable causes that must create their corresponding positive effects.

The True Path demands such an attitude of surrender. It is necessary that the personal self be given up unconditionally and absolutely, in thought as in action. The servant of Life lives not for self, but for the world, and in such devotion he consummates his liberation from the bleak and lonely ways of the struggling ego. Once the spiritual aspirant embarks wholeheartedly upon the True Path, his personality will begin to disappear as he proceeds toward becoming a transparent conduit of benevolence. This does not mean that he will lose his identity, however; to the contrary, he will expand it and add to it something infinitely more splendid. Such spiritual alchemy gives one a sense of the utmost security and certitude, imparting the most tremendous spiritual stimulus imaginable, and bestows upon the worthy person the privileged ability to channel powerful divine forces safely for the blessing of the world.

In ceasing to resist universal law, the spiritually-acquiescent person consciously takes up his rightful place as a tiny yet essential thread within the infinite and exquisitely intricate tapestry of life, and so begins to weave a new and harmonious expression in perfect uniformity with the ever-changing, ever-moving energy patterns of life. In divine affinity such an aligned individual is then able to effortlessly radiate wholesome spiritual energies for the healing and upliftment of all life that they touch; this is why all saints are healers. Saints incarnate or emerge upon Earth to act as outposts of divine force, and in order to maintain this privilege they are required to keep their *vessels* empty. Thus, as prepared instruments they are employed by the divine Will to conduct, step down and distribute spiritual energy within the lower worlds. Therefore, all those who would walk the True Path must possess not only righteous motivations, but also an unassuming and humble attitude that will ensure that their *vessels* remain open and empty.

The perfect examples of our saints demonstrate clearly that the True Path requires an unconditionally altruistic disposition that necessarily and spontaneously produces active service. The divine Spirit works through all such truly loving endeavours, no matter how seemingly mundane or trivial one's activities may appear to be. As Saint Theresa of Calcutta said, *"It is not the things that we do which count in the eyes of God, but how much love we put into doing them."* The Law of Love may seem paradoxical, for Love must be given in order to be received. If we would not lose a divine gift that we have gained, then we must give it away, and the impulse to serve selflessly springs from such spiritual understanding and from a genuine love of humanity and of life. Upon the path of spiritual progress, this impulse eventually becomes the overwhelming goal of all, and a growing proportion of the planetary population is today swiftly moving toward a desire to be of service. Such a benevolent attitude constitutes truly illumined understanding and reveals that in order to elicit real wisdom and its corresponding emancipation, one has to reach it through the whole of life, through an inclusive awareness that only unconditional Love can awaken. True understanding begets pure motive, and this allows the divine Spirit to operate through the prepared instrument—the personality—effortlessly, appropriately and joyfully in every moment. It is altruism—never egotism—that leads the aspirant to merge the lower self in the Universal Self, and it is to the aforementioned requirements—necessary to attain the One Goal—that candidates upon the True Path must devote themselves if they would court divine Revelation.

It may be seen, then, that the greatest blessing in the whole universe is the opportunity to serve, and the corresponding experience of spiritual realization upon the receipt of divine grace has always been just a pure thought away for humanity. Yet the majority of spiritual aspirants upon Earth today have failed to grasp the essential key to the truly divine life. Within the higher worlds there exists an infinite reservoir of benevolent force that is always ready and waiting to be downpoured into the physical plane when a suitable channel is constructed via the personality. A strong enough feeling of perfectly unselfish devotion provides such a channel, the response to which would be a descent of divine vitality resulting in a great strengthening and uplifting of the creator of the channel, plus the radiating all about that person of a powerful and beneficent influence for the helping of all life, affecting most positively the consciousness of mankind. Such functioning as a voluntary agent of grace is a blessed honour indeed, and having awakened divine inspiration within, the person who has caught even the slightest fragrance of that *manna from heaven* becomes most naturally impelled to proceed with the greatest enthusiasm upon the True Path to serve others with a holy reverence made possible by a heart enraptured by boundless Love. *"Such is the sweetness of deep delight of these touches of God, that one of them is more than a recompense for all the sufferings of this life, however great their number."*—St. John of the Cross.

✳ ✳ ✳

The path of selfless service—the way of true spiritual emancipation—is by far the most easy, joyful and quickest road leading back to the *Kingdom of God*. In every race and nation, in every clime and part of the world, and throughout the endless reaches of time, back into the limitless past, human beings have discovered the way that leads to liberation through helping others. They have trodden the True Path gladly, accepted its conditions, endured happily its disciplines and exemplified its virtues. They have rested back in confidence upon its realities, received its rewards, and, through its verities, they have realized the One Goal of Deliverance. Discovering that most cherished prize, they have entered into the *Joy of Heaven*, participated in the mysteries of Paradise, dwelled for a while in the glory of the divine Presence, and then always have they returned to the ways of the world, to serve. The testimony to the existence of this path is retained in the price-

less treasures of wisdom left behind by its witnesses who successfully transcended all desire for the personal self, and who
consequently penetrated into the ever-expanding world of true
meaning and divine purpose. The road to their ultimate triumph
began—as every individual must begin—with right understanding.

The bridge between the temporary human consciousness and
Cosmic Consciousness is built by the mind purified of erroneous
thinking; it is understanding that transforms us, not merely the
desire for change. Once a basic understanding of the great laws of
the universe has been gained, right attitude will certainly dawn
within us, and thus favorably adjusted in our perceptions of the
world, we shall delight in sharing our newly-discovered treasure
with and for others as we begin to tread the grandest and most fulfilling path of service. Upon the True Path, through a loving unification with the One Self in all, the protective sheath of egotism that
separates is gradually dissolved, and our consciousness is liberated as it becomes identified with all life.

Right understanding allows us to consciously and intelligently
embark upon the rich, colorful and varied adventure that life truly
is. The previously hidden effulgent light of the spiritual Sun will
then begin to emerge in bright and golden hue from behind the
clouds of past erroneous thinking habits, and will scintillate into
our conscious awareness, illuminating and dispelling our false
perceptions as it reveals the radiance of Reality. We then find ourselves safely upon the True Path, equipped with and protected by
our new understanding and awareness that so adjust our attitude
that, as we conduct our life in alignment with universal law, we
come to see that we can never again fall back into the cold and
lonely shadows of our ignorant selfhood.

* * *

Now, Servers, like all humanity, should do what they find
uplifting, what gives them a sense of real purpose. They simply
need to follow their joy, for in joy there is happiness, and where
there is happiness, spontaneous and spirited service will naturally
flow from a full and loving heart. Let Servers do whatever makes
the heart sing, and if ever they should find that their heart is out of
tune, then perhaps there is a new song to learn. The True Path is
never dull, for as we serve, we also learn. The greatest teacher will
inevitably be the best student, and it is well known to such a one

that the rate of learning is much enhanced upon the path of loving service.

Servers who have awakened in recognition of the wisdom in embarking upon the way of selfless service will soon come to comprehend the liberating Law of Allowance,[*] as they happily choose to live by it. In giving up all attachment to results, they may begin to clearly perceive that in and of themselves they may do nothing spiritually worthwhile. However, in removing the lower self from their world perspective, Servers will find that their very own divine Intelligence is able to shine through their unobstructed personality. In re-establishing their familiar attitude of perfect surrender to and trust in the omniscience of Life, they will again recall that it is only the divine Spirit that may truly serve at all: it serves itself in other seemingly individual manifestations of the One. This is, of course, a major revelation *and* disappointment as far as the ego is concerned, for during its entire life it has habitually delighted in accepting all credit afforded it with an alacrity born of perfect ignorance. In faithful allowance of what *is*, awakened Servers upon the right road to spiritual success cease in their struggling habits (which they may have adopted from humanity's example) as they recall their own innate wisdom that reminds them to *simply love*, and then to just let it be. Everything is then rightfully seen as perfect in the world, as it always has been; the Law of Cause and Effect governing the great pageantry of Creation and operating throughout every particle of the universe and every experience of life.

All awakened Servers will recall that it is the Greater Self—the divine Spirit—that is actually in command, and not the personality. Due to their past identification with the imitation ego and its self-created worldly illusions, many Servers have unwittingly turned away from a true friend and guide—their group-soul—which, as an adequately qualified and divinely-appointed representative of the Universal Mind, has ever been whispering gently and silently to them in its natural predilection to serve the world by way of their personality, patiently waiting for recognition and right response. The all-knowing, all-loving Spirit of Creation will always illumine the mind and heart of one who acts and works in accordance with its wise adjudication, and to follow that Spirit

---

[*]   Jesus alluded to this law—the honouring of which is so essential to true happiness—when he invited us to simply *"Let it be."*

wherever it may indicate is to walk the Lighted Way.

Awakened Servers who have, once again, found the True Path leading heavenward, offer a vital catalyst to others for their own spiritual advancement by affording them the most blessed opportunity to unite in service to the Divine Plan which, when acknowledged and accepted by the free-will decision of each individual, will raise their vibratory rate of consciousness and lead to progressive emancipation from the pain and suffering of the lower self.

＊ ＊ ＊

When we follow the natural urge of our innermost being and thus give of ourselves sincerely in helpfulness and in love, the Light of the Spirit is enkindled within us and we know that we are doing something right and good. In genuine service to other manifestations of the One Life, divine Love is bound by cosmic law to manifest, and it is through selfless charity that we may claim our rightful spiritual legacy: the realization and expression of our own latent divinity. If there ever was one solution to absolutely every problem throughout mankind's history, all the way up to the present, and on into Eternity, it must surely be...*serve, and keep serving; give, and never stop giving.* For it is in giving that we receive; such is the promise of the insuperable Law of Recompense that returns to the giver many times more than that which they originally gave from a loving heart.

The True Path is certain to lead the devout from the very darkest areas of life into those of empyreal radiance. The purpose, fulfilment, expanding revelation, ever-deepening joy and emancipation upon the road that rises up through all the luminous worlds of Spirit will be known to the one who serves others selflessly. That complete, intelligent and unconditional devotion and one-pointedness of mind that marks the awakened servants of all, provides a refuge in a world of turmoil, and they are as happy as they are divinely inspired to remain upon their chosen path until they arrive at that guaranteed liberation which culminates in complete equanimity, unalloyed peace and perfect holiness.

For such spiritual victors, it is the Truth which has become their saviour: the only saviour; it is the Truth that is their polestar leading homeward, while service is their sure means of return. The Truth is their valid passport back to the Blessed Land, and it ensures all happy travellers of their final release from enslavement to all worldly delusions. Truth—experienced wholly only in service to others—is to every wayfarer of life the only worthy nourishment for the personal spirit; it evinces Love in the one who serves which is refreshing and all-satisfying to the thirsting soul, and comforting to the yearning heart. Truth fills the one who is empty; in revealing divine promise, it restores hope and inspiration to the one who has become lost in a confused world, and it frees the person who is in bondage to self. Truth is the light at the end of the dark tunnel of all illusions born of the lower self. Every joy springs from the One Great Joy that is Truth. To seek and to find the Truth is the sole purpose of existence; it is the only spiritually worthwhile reality to live or to die for. As an everlasting, eternal spring, Truth forever flows inexorably throughout all Creation with the single intention of seeking to reveal its heart, which is Love, and this it does most perfectly in service to others.

As we offer ourselves up in service to the world, selflessly and unconditionally as surrendered instruments of the divine Will, we shall witness in reposed delight as the great boon beyond all limitation manifests in our lives as surely as the early sun smiles upon a fresh spring morning on a clear new day. Such a natural event is an inevitable result that we shall bring about by our inspired dedication to the good of all. By law, holy Revelation will evince itself as a corollary of that true understanding that we have now integrated into our lives; the ineffable joy of expanding spiritual emancipation will be realized due to our right attitude; and Heaven's ever-unfolding splendor will become an eternally-assured reality for us in accord with our wise resolution to love all equally.

"Whosoever would become great among you shall be your servant." —Mark 10:43

The Call to Service

THE TIME OF THE GREAT AWAKENING HAS COME. You who have chosen to lift your eyes from the darkness to the light are blessed to see the advent of a new day on the Earth. Because your heart has yearned to see peace where war has reigned, to show mercy where cruelty has dominated, and to know love where fear has frozen hearts, you are privileged to usher real healing to your world.

The Creator has chosen your hands to reach the lonely, your eyes to see innocence in the guilty, and your lips to utter words of comfort to the wounded. Let pain be no more! You have wandered in dark dreams for too long; now you must step into the light and stand for what you know to be true. Fear must be ended now, forever, and it is within your power to do so.

No one can find yourself but you. All of your answers are within you. You must now teach the lessons which you have learned. Your understanding has been given not only for yourself, but to guide a sore and tired world to a place of rest in a new consciousness.

Go forth then, and be a messenger of hope. Point the way to healing by walking in great fullness. Your brothers and sisters will follow, and as you pass beyond the portal of limitation you will be united and reunited with all who seemed to be lost. There is no loss in the Creator. Choose the path of forgiveness, and you will weep tears of joy for the goodness you find in all.

Go forth and live the life of the radiant soul that you are. You are important, you are needed, and you are worthy. Never allow the dark cloak of fear to hide the light from your view. You were not born to fail; you are destined to succeed. The hope of the world has been planted in your breast, and you are assured of success as you stand for the One Who created you.

The Children of Light, Alan Cohen.

Although awakened Servers—*The Children of Light*—demonstrate love and kindness to all, it should be remembered that they are also bringers of destruction, for they are charged with the responsibility of clearing the weeds of ignorance from the pathways of Earth so that new growth may blossom forth. The collective force of their awesome and fiery blessings will shatter and dispel the planetary gloom that today hangs over the spirit of mankind like a burial shroud. Servers *"come not to bring peace, but the sword,"* and all those idealists in the world who may have built up a preconditioned holy image of the character of the typical awakened Server today—perhaps modelled upon the joy-intoxicated saints of the past—may be disappointed! In fact, Servers who form the frontline of change in these times are necessarily a great deal more militant than outwardly saintly, for in order to achieve their goal they must, without reservation, charge forth to rend asunder that great veil of delusion that has been forged and maintained by evil minds and which, by means of *vibratory imprisonment,* has prevented humanity from knowing any real freedom, peace or happiness for so long.

It should obviously not be expected that the forces of darkness, having reigned upon Earth for so many ages, will surrender their dominion without great resistance. Consequently, the years that lie just ahead may appear awful and devastating to secular vision, yet seen by the eyes of the soul—which can truly see—they will be recognized to be pregnant with the power of justice and righteousness. The urgently needed cleansing of the whole planet will include a torrential inrush of divine light that will blind and overwhelm those who are unprepared, but will fill those who are ready with unsurpassed elation as they are glorified by the unveiled Truth. The one great enemy of Truth is self. Therefore, peril, regret, fear and dread lie ahead only for those who harbour the evil of selfishness, for mirrors line the way.

Adequate warning has been given to every soul repeatedly over numerous incarnations: *"Prepare ye! O prepare! for the Kingdom is at hand"* Yet still today humanity typically chooses pain as its teacher instead of love. Perhaps many will not believe the truth of the times until their familiar, comfortable but redundant reality begins to collapse all around them. Mostly, mankind will be forced to learn hard but necessary lessons during the coming upheavals, while those who see and understand will bide their time with discernment in usefulness and service as they await the Harvest Time in knowing anticipation. Their patience and fortitude in active service is certain to avail them of the tender-sweet fruit of the long-awaited divine Promise.

As Servers procure the life-raft of love and goodwill for the family of humanity, they will remain afloat during the coming tidal floods of planetary cleansing. Servers may take further comfort in the incontrovertible fact that the vast collective intelligence that is their group-soul lovingly watches over them always. Although these great guiding and protecting entities may remain just out of range of ordinary perception, should Servers look deeply within their hearts, past all doubts, and should they really trust their innermost senses and so heed them well, they will perceive the reality of the existence and proximity of their spiritual family. Indeed, divine response to the need for guidance and protection in demanding circumstances is often magically instantaneous, and to this fact a growing number of faithful individuals today bear witness. Even though their eyes may still be partially veiled, directed and protected by hidden yet ever-present divine Helpers, Servers will be surely guided toward the mountain top that marks the final attainment of their long pilgrimage. At the appointed time everything will fall perfectly into place, and every awakened Server will know what to do. All loving hearts are assured of a safe passage through the oncoming tempest; by following the inner polestar that glimmers always, even in the darkest night, every Server will find his way home.

However, the spiritual 'home' of the indwelling life is not a location, but a state of Grace; one which is earned only by loving others. Once Servers have awakened and consequently reconsecrated themselves in service to their fellows who have become lost in a world of painful illusions, they will realize that they do not need to go anywhere at all, and that they are actually able to bring their home-vibration to Earth in order to share its healing solace with all.

In thus selflessly dedicating their unique gifts and talents to the present divine Cause upon Earth, Servers form an essential world infrastructure of educators, artists, healers, seers, planetary stewards, new scientists, etc. They teach the Law of Love, of Harmony and Health; they understand and live by the Law of Creativity and, therefore, that of Evolution. They assist in the removal of all that obscures clear perception of these laws and which, therefore, diminishes the experience of divine Reality. Awakened Servers understand well that the present world crisis demands not workshops, courses and lectures, but *active participation* in the creation of the New World. Many of these Servers are presently still working underground—silently and occultly—for they have recognized that so many *words* have been spoken and recorded for the masses throughout history by spiritual teachers, yet still selfishness, disease and immorality prevail upon Earth. Nevertheless, they understand well the need of the hour and, as a group, they are today beginning to break their long and necessary silence with a New Song.

That Great Song of the Spirit, which is ever new, has in past been heard by certain privileged members of the human race singing through those precious few devoted hearts filled with the joy of righteousness in holy service. Such rare and compassionate individuals have earnestly endeavoured to take onto their own shoulders the various burdens of mankind. Usually rendered alone and little understood by most, their task has been a formidable one, yet in maintaining a dutiful attitude, the divine Spirit helped to lift their load, dispel their pain and ease their forward passage. Thus, throughout long ages of willing toil and struggle upon Earth, they have diligently sought by example to show the Way to humanity in the hope that a few might follow. As solitary wayfarers—tiny points of light in the darkness—their load has been a ponderous one of loving sacrifice. Yet such sacrifice will soon be rightfully recognized by all successful Servers as nothing less than the greatest honour, for the concluding phase of their great journey has arrived, and the fruits of their labour will shortly be revealed to all as they rise up in unprecedented numbers in order to ensure the success of this present and most important phase of the Divine Plan for planet Earth. All awakening Servers today are beginning to recognize that their long, hard and often painful labour of love for this world is almost complete, and that the Aquarian age will not be an era of sacrifice and suffering, but a time of joy. It is they who shall take down the Piscean cross of crucifixion and rejoice in the new way of spontaneous love and harmonious, purposeful cooperation on Earth. Presently, a magnificent experience of *déjà vu* will be known by every wearied pilgrim as the long-awaited moment finally arrives, dispelling all fatigue, evincing the imminent verdict of countless lives and lifetimes, signifying the end of a long cycle, and ushering in a bright new era for mankind.

All unawakened Servers are now called to *remember*, to take up their positions and to use their innate abilities for helping others in order that in so doing they may become conscious agents of the New Spirit and an active part of today's expanding consciousness around the planet. Karma is created by what is done or neglected to be done based upon what has been *understood*. Therefore, Servers are duty-bound to act upon the highest truth that they have recalled. Knowledge is a responsibility as well as a gift and, as keepers of the keys to New Life, Servers are exhorted by the Lords of Evolution who oversee the Divine Plan upon Earth to apply themselves wisely in world service. They are today urged to wield the hidden forces that are available to them in order to generate positive causes for the common good, thereby bringing an end to the illusion of separation by manifesting the New World Consciousness.

The responsibility for appropriate action and effort to reach others with important and contemporary information rests upon the shoulders of all awakening Servers today. Additionally, dedicated assistance from mankind is a prerequisite if the approaching planetary upheavals are to be attenuated, and Servers must do everything in their power to inspire and elicit that assistance. It is our *time* for which the great spiritual Hierarchies are today calling; it is our practical *activity* and *skill* that are required to aid all those who can be assisted; it is our *charity* and *love* that are so vitally needed, not only as a balm for the wounds of mankind, but also, and more importantly, for the dissemination of required and contemporary spiritual education and truly helpful guidance. It is our *service* which is demanded by today's intensifying world conditions in order to facilitate contact with all those who are interested in joining together to contribute toward that which must and will be achieved. It is our *selfless meditation, inspiration,* inner and outer *devotion* and *invocation* that will construct the channel through which the New Spirit may enter this world. Great pain and suffering may be avoided in the immediate future by the acquisition of a true understanding of today's climactic circumstances, and the intelligent application of that understanding in daily life.

Generally upon Earth, it is only when we experience, through ample suffering, that there is no happiness to be found in this world of desire and self-seeking that we turn wholeheartedly to the divine Spirit and call sincerely for help. When we convince that Spirit that we wish to live, as we are able, in alignment with the purposes of the Divine Plan, then assistance is conferred from the unseen worlds. Sincere and selfless invocation guarantees an inflow of spiritual force, and divine succor is to be found upon the True Path in the most unlikely places.

* * *

All awakened Servers are realists, they do not possess the quixotic and dreamy psychologies that are so prevalent today within the New Age movement, and which give rise to the vast majority of imitation spirituality by furnishing grandiose but false promises of paradise, free for all. Someone once said that there is no elevator to success, we all have to take the stairs. No New Age healing method, religious doctrine, technique of self-improvement, enlightened guru, or salvation by extraterrestrials in spaceships, will liberate or make a person more spiritual. Individuals may rise up from where they are only by using their own past and present experiences as a springboard into greater understanding and awareness, by *giving* of what they have in service to the world, and by *loving* others, no less and no more.

Applicable throughout the birth of the New World, and in accordance with the new laws of the Aquarian age, the following statement of fact should be afforded due attention by all serious aspirants for harvest: *should an individual be unprepared to happily and spontaneously give of everything that they are able in order to serve the common good; if there is any measure of fear, self-regard and, therefore, reservation in that person, then they necessarily exclude themselves from the ranks of the true servants of the world, and so they cannot be a part of the One Divine Work upon Earth today; there can be no compromise in genuine spiritual service. Furthermore, in the times ahead, all that which is held to oneself, anything that is not offered selflessly in service to others, and everything which is not contributed toward the One Great Cause will be taken away.*

Those who do not genuinely love and therefore seek to help humanity cannot gain entry into the New World; those who live only for self will be unable to receive the Aquarian grace, while those who willingly give their life for others will be lifted up by the New Spirit. Let all Servers, therefore, remember always that there is but one sure road ahead, and once they have found that road and seen where it leads, may nothing trouble, shake or disturb them from following it homeward. Treading the Lighted Way brings rewards that are everlasting. There is no need for doubt. Doubt is the enemy of progress, and should Servers meet a foe at some point along their path who appears too formidable for them, they need not falter, for all the Hosts of Heaven will stand in their defence. Due to the inherent divine solidarity that is always present amongst those who live in harmony with the benign Forces of Good, the person who sincerely treads the True Path is automatically aided and protected throughout life's vicissitudes by the invisible benevolence of ever-attending divine Guides. Conversely, the person upon the path of service to self is much more prone to random 'accidents' and setbacks; they may find no haven from the gales and tempests of life's often seemingly cruel conditions.

The light of the New World Consciousness will inevitably dawn brighter for each individual in direct proportion to the degree of which they give from their hearts for the helping of others. In so doing, the truth of the times will reveal itself to them from within: *"And in these hours be anxious not about your speech; you need not think of what to say; for, lo, the Holy Breath will overshadow you and give you words to say."*—Jesus. To share the truth of the times with everyone is to begin to tread the True Path, each moment drawing nearer to the Portal of Liberation. Service, however, may only be rendered where and when it is requested; one cannot free others who are still engrossed in the limitations and conditions of the old world consciousness and its thought-forms by attempting to pull them loose through mere force of mind or emotion. A great many souls will— consciously or unconsciously—choose *not* to take advantage of the unprecedented opportunity offered them at the forthcoming Harvest Time. Such ones may be recognized by their *vibration*, and their free will must be honoured, however unfortunate or painful their choice may seem to be. Their turn will surely come around upon another world at some future occasion. When Servers are not heard or openly received they would do well not to tarry long, but instead venture forward to sow the seeds of Truth generously, for fertile minds do exist in the world that would happily court the light, serve the Divine Plan and so receive the New Spirit.

It is time for every Server in the world to deftly sweep aside all divisions, dualities and separative illusions, and to pool resources in order to embrace today's great opportunity to assist Mother Earth in her rebirth. Planetary midwifery is a much needed and sought after qualification and service at this special time, and one that necessarily requires a perfectly united consciousness in order to assure success. No group of people may work as a unit unless they genuinely love and serve one another; divine forces cannot flow through the group if there exists any disharmony amongst its members. All Servers are hereby called forth to consciously resume their spiritual duty in the world, to step forward to be an example to others in these "testing times" as they assist in the unfoldment of the *Destiny of Ages*, for only together as One may we usher in the grace and glory of the New World.

Opportunity has been given by those invisible Servants of the race upon the inner side of life, and they now await the active and positive response to their call. They are watching lovingly, patiently and enthusiastically, and remain ever attentive to and supportive of all sincere efforts made toward aiding in the unfoldment of the Divine Plan, in the anchoring and diffusion of the new Aquarian energies upon Earth, and in the expeditious preparation for the imminent birth of a New Age. These Great Beings are today poised above the planet, as it were, and ready to activate the further inpouring of Love and healing force for the good of mankind. Receptivity is directly dependent upon a righteous and selfless attitude, and the prompt, positive and altruistic action of those who are aware and ready.

The new call to world salvage has gone out, and many today are responding in various ways. Motives are often mixed, and response is frequently inspired by a desire for personal safety, progress, recognition and aggrandizement. Servers must rise above such selfishness, for such reactions are at this particular time greatly complicating the call to service while simultaneously illustrating the contemporary veracity of an old admonition: *"Many are called but few are chosen."* Today's call to service stresses emphatically its invitation for appropriate action. The greater message to all Servers in the world is: *seek, get understanding, remember, assemble, purify, prepare together, and be of service to your human family.*

During their present and conclusive struggle for the establishment of righteousness on Earth, may all Servers forget not those precious glimpses of impending glory given them in past moments of divine contact, and may they seek always to inspire others by reminding them of the promised hour which shall presently open the door to the New World so that all who are ready may enter in. May Servers allow no obstacle to hinder them, but only strengthen their resolve to forge ahead with the virtue of renewed determination. May temptation, fear and doubt neither deter nor delay them from helping humanity to rise up into the New Light, and in so doing rise up themselves. *"If fear should stop us in the middle of the road, we would hear only ridicule from the voices of the night, but if we reach the mountain peak bravely we shall join the heavenly spirits in songs of triumph and joy."*—Kahlil Gibran.

The headstrong winds of ignorance that thrash and buffet the seas of Earthly consciousness today demand a sturdy sail and sure navigation in order for Servers to keep their fleet on course. The success of their grand voyage depends upon the dedicated hearts of each crew member, their clarity of intent and unity of spirit. Each member of the group is a valuable asset to the party. With eyes fixed upon the rising Sun of the New Day and with hearts united, together Servers are assured of victory and the long-anticipated Final Liberation.

Afterword

THE LORD BUDDHA *was once staying in a forest in Kosambi, India, where he took a few leaves into his hand, and asked of his disciples: "What do you think, O bhikkus? Which is more — these few leaves in my hand or the leaves in the forest over there?"*

"Sir, very few are the leaves in the hand of the Blessed One," a disciple replied, "but indeed the leaves in the forest over there are very much more abundant."

The Buddha continued, "Even so, bhikkus, of what is known to me I have told you only a little; what I have not told you is very much more. And why have I not told you these things? Because they are not useful, they are not fundamentally connected with the spiritual holy life, and will not lead you to Nirvana. That is why I have not told you these things."

The Buddha was not interested in discussing unnecessary metaphysical questions that might create imaginary problems and endless speculation. He considered such topics *"a wilderness of opinion."* Similarly, and for two very good reasons, this present work leaves out much that is being avidly discussed, researched, written about and taught today with regard to the dawning New Age of Aquarius.

Firstly, even a thousand treatises of encyclopedic magnitude could not convey all that is transpiring in the world, the solar system and beyond, and which is directly related to either Servers or the Divine Plan for planet Earth at this time. Consequently, an outline of a subject such as the one taken up in this book must necessarily remain synoptic and, therefore, in a sense, incomplete.

Secondly, much that falls within the very wide parameters of New Age thinking today, while often fascinating and quite thrilling, tends to be superfluous with regard to the immediate needs in the world. Amongst the plethora of new information that is currently available, there exist all kinds of very colorful enticements, and these may conduce toward restless excitement, convoluted perception, contagion and, therefore, unnecessary distraction from the most essential and pertinent issues of the day.

The Truth is, has ever been, and always will be simple; indeed, its essence is contained in one very fundamental yet profound statement, namely that *Love is the greatest aid to healing and spiritual progress.* In compiling this somewhat technical volume we have, on occasion, found ourselves wondering if its exposures might pose certain risks to some minds that may tend to become idealistically

169

attached to the ideas and ideals which it contains. We have experienced some concern at the possibility that we might be unintentionally responsible for helping to create new conceptual prisons for seekers of Truth. With this in mind, the following wisdom is offered from the Tao Te Ching: *"That which can be conveyed in words is merely a relative conception; although names and concepts have been applied to it, the subtle truth is indescribable."*—Lao Tzu.

Lest certain individuals fall into those identical entanglements that have obstructed clear and true spiritual vision in every age and culture, it is tempting for us to suggest that once the reader has understood and become inspired by the factual concepts expounded within this book, they might do well to forget about them altogether and simply practise unconditional love in their lives, for as the Buddha has averred: *"All is Samsara* [illusion].*"* To the unveiled eyes of one who has become enlightened by the simple Truth, and so who sees, with perfect clarity, things just as they are, phenomenal life is recognized to be but an intricate network of moving energy patterns, rising and passing away; nothing in this world is permanent or, therefore, Real.

It has been said before that philosophers die confused, separated from the Truth by their own grasping minds. Complex philosophies and ideas serve to scatter one's energy and focus in the moment, and lead to confusion. However, when we cease in our struggling, when we unreservedly trust life's processes and abide in acceptance and unconditional love for other life-forms, all that which is pertinent in the present instant is revealed to us; perfection of the moment is realized, while all our past mental constructs, subjective identifications of matter and phenomena, and of all conditioning factors relating thereto are seen as empty, devoid of substance, like ripples on a lake or moonbeams reflected in a looking-glass.

Wake-up calls, imitation egos, veils, portals and programs—these are all conceptual tools that attempt to confer an idea of certain esoteric dynamics that are ultimately beyond intellectual grasp; they are but indicators, signposts upon the way to the Greater Life. It should be remembered always that while such realities may be relevant on certain levels of *Samsara*, they are also ephemeral and so cease to exist upon others, as the developing point of consciousness—the soul—moves ever onward and inward upon its journey of progressive spiritual attainment and emancipation from all conceptual creations and transitory illusions belonging to the lower worlds.

It is our earnest prayer that the elucidations herein revealed are recognized for what they are, and that they do not become yet another substitute for Reality, which can only be *experienced*, never conceptualized. It is our wish that the principles and ideas that we have described will not be seen as an excuse for ceasing the necessary, joyful and eternal process of seeking further and higher, and it is our hope that our vision will ultimately help Servers and humanity alike to reach that most sacred place of pure, unconditional love where time touches Eternity, where the individual heart synchronizes and beats with the Universal Heart, and where the simple and unchanging Holy Truth may be *known*.

An ongoing Web forum presently exists to discuss the topics revealed in our first two books. Other writings that expand upon and complement the books are also available to subscribers. To apply for subscription to the Gateway forum, send a request to:

The-Gateway-subscribe@yahoogroups.com

Reviewing Recommendations

IN ORDER TO ACQUIRE A THOROUGH UNDERSTANDING of the causes and effects behind today's global transformations, it is recommended that the serious student obtain a copy of *The New Call* available from ourselves. In addition, the following books, movies and music are complementary to *Servers of the Divine Plan*. They serve to enhance the vision received by ourselves and will help to expand the knowledge and awareness of the studious seeker. Those entries that relate specifically to the subject matter of this book are marked by an asterisk (*).

A sound occult understanding will also be of invaluable assistance to the aspirant who plans to consciously enter the New World and to help others do the same. Therefore, unmarked book titles have also been included in the list. In addition to covering adequately the hidden side of personal relationships and the human microcosm—the inner constitution of humankind—these volumes offer most relevant and useful instruction about those unchanging spiritual principles and natural laws which guide and govern all the spheres within this octave of the universe.

Books

A Gift from Daniel—Karen Alexander
Astral Body, The—A E Powell
Causal Body, The—A E Powell
Celestine Prophecy, The—James Redfield *
ET 101—Jho Zoev *
From Bethlehem to Calvary—Alice Bailey
Hidden Side of Things, The—C W Leadbeater
Light Emerging—Barbara A Brennan
Masters and the Path, The—C W Leadbeater
Mental Body, The—A E Powell
Only Planet of Choice, The (*Chapters 1,7 & 8*)—Phyllis Schlemmer *
Preparing for Contact—Lyssa Royal & Keith Priest *
Prism of Lyra, The—Lyssa Royal & Keith Priest *
Star Born, The—Brad Steiger *
Starseed Transmissions, The—Ken Carey *
Strangers Among Us—Ruth Montgomery *
Tenth Insight, The—James Redfield *
Third Millennium, The—Ken Carey *

Movies

Phenomenon—starring John Travolta *
Powder—starring Sean Patrick Flanery *
The Matrix—starring Keanu Reeves *
K-PAX—starring Kevin Spacey, Jeff Bridges *

Music

Novus Magnificat (*Track 1 - 26 minutes*)—by Constance Demby *

Introducing
The New Call

TODAY, MANKIND STANDS WITNESS upon the eve of a great world transition. An unprecedented global metamorphosis is presently underway in preparation for a momentous leap in consciousness which the whole planet is about to take.

As a result of the Earth's entry into the age of Aquarius and due to the new life-energies that are flooding the planet, every human being is today faced with a critical choice that shall greatly affect both the present course of their life and their future spiritual journey, throughout incalculable incarnations.

NOW IS THE TIME TO PREPARE

THE NEW CALL . . .

Offers indispensable *keys to awakening* that are required to unlock the door of opportunity leading from the old age to the New.

Reveals how success may be guaranteed at the forthcoming Harvest Time.

Clarifies the obscurities and eradicates the unnecessary complexities that have grown up around New Age thinking.

Unshrouds the sinister side of the New Age movement as well as its divine promise.

Contains everything that mankind needs to understand in order to be prepared for that which lies just a little way ahead for us all.

Softcover may be purchased at http://www.1stbooks.com/bookview/16158

Or available free for download on http://www.thenewcall.org/book_download.htm

INNER TEACHINGS

WHEREVER WE LOOK TODAY within the spiritual supermarket there is restlessness, glamour and excitement, an eager pursuit for self-liberation, self-empowerment or 'ascension' from this world, the practice of low-grade psychism and an anxious fleeing from pain and responsibility—all in the name of spirituality.

As the long-prophesied influx of new light continues to enter our world, darkness is necessarily accentuated, and today the dawning light of the new Aquarian age is throwing shadows in all directions. The result? A great plethora of exaggeration, misinformation and imitation spirituality.

As stimulating psychic forces are being released and made available to mankind on an unprecedented scale, the unsuspecting, hasty and unenlightened are exhibiting their new abilities with remarkable alacrity, prematurely stepping forward to inaugurate themselves to the general public as spiritual teachers, healers and masters of wisdom.

These new teachers often offer fake spiritual gems that may appear to sparkle in the beginning, but soon fade and become lacklustre, along with the temporary satisfaction which may have been initially gleaned from them, while simultaneously they serve only to lead aspirants further and further away from the simple Truth.

However, that Truth is ever present and accessible by those who know where to look, and so who are able to find the Golden Key that unlocks the door to New Life.

* * *

At the end of every world cycle, a fresh and unadulterated form of the *Universal Doctrine*—or *Gnosis*—makes its reappearance on Earth in order to call in from the fields, before the Harvest Time, all those who are able to understand and apply it in their lives, and so meet the requirements of the latest cyclic opportunity for spiritual Deliverance.

The much needed rekindling of the Perennial Wisdom-Teaching of the Avatars in times of spiritual darkness signifies an informed effort to replace the plethora of misinterpretations, distortions and falsifications that will have inevitably spread throughout the world's religions and spiritual traditions over the centuries. It is, therefore, an important part of a truly religious endeavour to reestablish the Truth in the world and to thus contribute toward sounding the Final Call to humanity at the end of an age prior to the necessary planetary cleansing.

The word *Gnosis* is derived from the Greek language and means *Knowledge of God*, or *Divine Knowledge*. The Gnosis itself is Living Wisdom, unobtainable through the use of the intellect alone. However, when the earnest seeker of Truth utilizes the mental faculty in the right way, for the right reasons and in combination with the heart, he may be brought into contact with the Living Body that is Gnosis by way of the printed letter of the Law.

Although the Universal Knowledge that is of the Gnosis constitutes the foundation of every true religion, it has been expunged or, at best, grossly distorted in all those religious traditions that still exist today.

Presently, very few people in the world possess the vital Key that is Pure Gnosis, and this is one of the reasons why there is so much confusion, distraction, futility and sham spirituality abroad at this frantic time on the planet. Yet this very same Key has been discovered and used by every great spiritual luminary throughout Earth's history. All of these enlightened individuals found the One True Path that leads directly to the summit of Life, and in embarking upon the Lighted Way, they managed to bypass the multitudinous enticements and snares in the world of delusion to arrive safely Home. Today, we seek to free genuine candidates for harvest from all superfluous hubbub by placing before them esoteric facts that are as old as the planet, yet which have been re-presented in a modern format, taking into consideration today's grand opportunity as well as the new and adjusted laws of the Aquarian age.

* * *

It has been stated in the Hatha Yoga Pradapika: "*It* [yoga] *gives liberation to Yogis and bondage to fools.*" Similarly, and with regard to The Pure Gnosis, we would say that it may be liberating for earnest and mature seekers on the Path but onerous and thus potentially detrimental for less dedicated and, therefore, unprepared aspirants.

In times past, the Inner Teachings of the Universal Doctrine were given only to Initiates of genuine Mystery Schools, where stringent tests had to be passed before entrance to the Divine Mysteries was permitted. We are offering such information today only to those who are ready because we are in the "end times."

Due to the revelatory and uncompromising esoteric nature of that which is given in our advanced writings, they are reserved only for those serious and intelligent spiritual aspirants who know how to knock aright and so who already possess the key that unlocks the door.

"Let him who seeks continue seeking until he finds. When he finds he will become troubled, and when he becomes troubled he will be astonished... ."—Jesus, The Gnostic Gospel of Thomas.